ORAL SEX

Drive your man crazy

GODDESS OF SEX

Dylan Summers

ORAL SEX

Drive your man crazy

All the Keys and Secrets to Sex, Sensuality and Passion.

Pseudonym: Dylan Summers

Dylan Summers

I dedicate this book to you:

....

Goddess of Pleasure,

Sex, Sensuality and Passion.

Because everything you need is inside you.

I will glad to help you get that

Great Goddess inside you.

<u>CONTACT</u>

saraburillomoliner@gmail.com

Author`s Facebook:
https://www.facebook.com/SaraBurilloMolinero?fref=ts

ORAL SEX: Drive your man crazy
Sara Burillo

© 2017 Sara Burillo
Translation: Julia Simandan

AUTHOR'S BOOKS:

→ How to attract, seduce, captivate and influence others

→ Anxiety, Somebody help me!!

→ Discover your talent and make it your business

→ Kybalion: Discover the Law of Attraction

→ Goddess of Sex: drive your man crazy "Dylan Summers"

ABOUT THE AUTHOR:

Sara Burillo was born in a village in the province of Burgos, Spain. There she was raised and grew up till she moved to Marbella (province of Malaga), where she would spend her final adolescent years and adult life. Her career in Psychology aroused her passion to help others overcome their problems. She has done a lot of Pro research to find new therapies in different fields, among others; anxiety, stress, depression, fear of speaking in public, bring out hidden talents, the search for happiness, the art of influencing others, techniques to make new friends and keeping mental stability in any area or ambience. Now she is embarked on issues such as chronic pain, sexual disorders, tinnitus and works related to spirituality, as well as improvement in self esteem, just to mention a few. The versatility of this author brings us to the current spiritual questions from an introductory book to Kybalion and the keys that make up the Law of Attraction.

COMPLIMENTS:

I am mainly grateful to Julia Simandan, my dearest translator, her time and magic she projects; because without her it would not have been possible to sell the books that today I have translated into the English language, and because she is a person who has managed to stay in my mind even through the passage of time, because without realizing it she makes people love her. All other compliments go to my parents, my brothers and sisters and friends; even though the most special part of this goes directly to my loyal companion, my already older four legged canine called Arquímedes; who accompanies me day and night, bearing my own monologues while I decide which information is worthwhile, and who makes me take walks and breathe in the air from the woods of my hometown so as to analyze all the information that I write and that of which I will write later on. Without him, the ideas would not flow the way they do, and the books surely would not even have half of the magic that I try to achieve for you, my dear reader, so that they can serve their purpose from hereon.

COMPLIMENTS TO THE READER:
It is here when I say to you, reader, not only do I want to speak to you of the gratitude I feel for you, but also something more. I want to tell you that you are the link to each and every one of my thoughts that were channeled. If you would not exist, this book would not have been created. So, read it as what it is, a written creation specifically and with all my love and tender care for you; with the hope that you enjoy while reading it and that it can serve in part or completely so you can be as happy as you wish to be...Thank you for existing.

INDEX

1

WHAT DOES GIVING PLEASURE TO A MAN EXACTLY MEAN

"Sex is not the answer, it is the question. The answer is YES".

Anonymous

Men especially enjoy oral sex (fellatio), it's the reason why the majority of them ask to have it done. But oral sex, just as any other sexual practice, requires a certain skill. We might feel a little insecure at the time of practicing it if we're inexperienced in this field. Therefore, throughout this manual, we'll be giving some basic ideas on how to practice oral sex satisfactorily on one hand. On the other, we'll see how we can use THE MAGIC in this marvelous practice.

Sexual relations, and therefore also oral sex, are based on a series of basic pillars: the five senses. Sight, smell, touch, hearing and taste. Apart from these, there's the already mentioned MAGIC, which is no more and no less than the energy that we'll use in the act. The latter is far from simple and because of it we'll discuss it in continuous occasions, just as there is a specific book on this subject (at the end of this book you can see the title). Each one of them are to be considered at the time of having sexual relations, because it'll be the combination of all of them that will create a unique and unrepeatable erotic situation.

Oral sex could appear to us as something simple: insert the penis into the mouth and go up and down. This technique might be all right for our first time, but if we want our man to enjoy each fellatio to its fullest, we must improve our subtlety, craftiness and technique. We'll discover how to play with the rhythms, with suction techniques, with our lips, our tongue... At the end of this manual we can get all our repertoire to achieve a superb and unforgettable experience.

Throughout this book, we will also see the different erogenous areas that can be stimulated during oral sex, the positions we can adopt, the roles we can play, and some references and solutions to the most common problems. In addition, five exercises on how to perform oral sex to serve as an example, will be explained in detail.

2

QUALMS ABOUT PRACTICING ORAL SEX

"Sex is a part of nature, and I get along with nature beautifully".

Marilyn Monroe

We may not like or refuse to perform oral sex to a man. This could possibly result in confrontations and arguments with our partner, since our partner will try to make us change our mind. There are various reasons why we could be avoiding this type of sexual practice, but the important thing is to have good communication with our partner. If we don't feel comfortable performing oral sex, our partner should know about it. This would avoid bad misunderstandings and unpleasant situations where we might feel forced to do something we don't want to do. Surely our partner could do something so, gradually, we'd feel more confident with this technique, and if not, he'll have to accept it and look for other types of practices equally satisfying.

Although it's totally permissable not wanting to practice oral sex, and no one tries to make anyone feel judged or feel obligated to do it, there are going to be some aspects that may change the conception that we may have about oral sex. If that is the case and we achieve to change those prejudices, congratulations! If on the contrary, the rejection is determined due to other types of circumstances, it doesn't matter, as it's been said before, there are many other techniques for seeking pleasure and not falling into monotony.

Oral sex wasn't always as popular as it is today. Right now, if a survey of the masculine population would be made, it would surely be the preferred practice by the majority of men. However, some decades ago, oral sex was seen as something typical of the "women of the night", something considered immoral or dirty. That's why many older couples haven't practiced this technique; or if they have done, it was very seldom and they've concealed it as well.

This vision about oral sex has been changing over the years, since society now is much more open sexually. Nevertheless, there are still women who continue to see oral sex as something immoral, beneath dignity, degrading, etc. This is also influenced by the religious aspect, which conceives sexual relations only for procreating. Therefore, getting pleasure is frowned upon. What's more, these judgments will be strengthened if we think that we're the only species that has sex to obtain pleasure, and the rest of the animals only have sex in order to reproduce.

But this isn't true, it's been shown that other species

also copulate in situations where it's impossible for the female to get pregnant, like for example, when she's already pregnant or when she's in her nursing stage. And more specifically, there are animals that have oral sex as mere playful behavior, such as the bonobos (formerly called pygmy chimpanzees), fruit bats or dolphins which have also been seen with sexual behavior between individuals of the same sex.

Another reason why we might object doing oral sex to a man is because we see the penis as something "dirty". And this is not so unreasonable, as there are men who don't maintain a proper hygiene of that area, and so it ends up smelling bad due to traces of urine, sweat and semen. If this is our only setback, we have an easy solution: wash it. It's also true though, to tell a guy that he should clean his intimate area because the smell is unpleasant could be rather uncomfortable and even hurt him. Nevertheless, we can turn to games and foreplay that can help us with our mission. For example, why not start by sharing a relaxing shower? We can wash ourselves together and that way we make sure that his genitals are clean.

Another aspect to deal with would be the pubic hair. If there is a lot of it, this makes them sweat more and the smell impregnates much easier. To solve this issue, we can tell him that we prefer a shaven penis, that way his male parts stand out more, that it seems more exciting to us, etc. What's more, hairless genitals allows us to use more techniques during oral sex, how to play with his testicles, as well as avoid getting hair in our mouth and cause obstruction during the act. However, he doesn't need to shave completely, simply trimming the pubic area a little and the testicles would be sufficient, and with just this measure, we'll notice a big difference.

In the same area as the above, we may be afraid of catching diseases. If we don't get it out of our heads that the penis is the organ from where men urinate, and we see it as a dirty or disgusting organ, most likely we won't want to, for anything in the world, ever put it into our mouth. As a first measure, we'd have to turn to the previous point and clean it really well. Nevertheless, no matter how well a penis has been soaped down and taken care of, the risk of catching a sexually transmitted infection still exists. For this, the best precaution that we can take is by using condoms. There are condoms specifically designed for oral sex, that are much finer and with different flavors. If in the event that the man starts to be more than a sexual companion (going on to being a steady partner), we can ask him to have a test done for sexually transmitted infections, making it clear that we ask this simply so we can relax and be able to do anything without fears. He'll understand. In the event that he doesn't want to do it, we mustn't forget that the person that really matters is oneself, so if he doesn't want to do it, we shouldn't have to be exposed to any risks for anyone. In this latter event, if we still want to go ahead and continue with oral sex, it would be very important if not essential to use measures already mentioned.

We must always remember that it's advisable to use condoms whenever the man is not well known or if we're in an open relationship, since we don't know if he's used a condom with other partners. Although at first it may be a measure that doesn't convince us, health is the main thing.

All these prejudices that we've talked about may

keep us back in our sexual life. Even though we're unaware of it, these beliefs hinder and distance us from having a fulfilling sexual life.

Lastly, some women consider oral sex as something very intimate, and prefer not practicing oral sex unless they have an emotional attachment to the man. This decision is totally acceptable, the only thing that we must bear in mind is that some men may not like our position; and like we've said and don't get tired repeating it, here what is really important is that we feel good and that we place our needs first. We shouldn't have to feel bad or feel obligated to do what we don't want to do because of it. If we see that our date has a wrong idea about what we're going to do, we simply let him know ahead of time that we don't like to practice oral sex with a person that isn't a steady partner and we encourage him in doing other types of practices. If in the event he doesn't understand or even gets angry, again we say that the important thing is oneself and that there are not thousands but millions of men to choose from.

Now we're going to present a series of beliefs and

meditate upon them in the event that they are a part of our lives:

1.- **My religion doesn't allow it**: Without seeking to bring down your own beliefs in regard to the religion you are practicing at this time, let me tell you that no human being should tell you and much less impose on you what you can or cannot do. If there is anyone who should decide is you alone with your beliefs, not your religion, which is something different. Believing in God is one thing, and joining together with other people and making out a set of rules to follow according on how to interpret the words of God in whom you believe is something completely different. What do we mean by this? Not that you should abandon your religion, but to expose that you alone should lead and choose your life, not a set of laws or rules made by a group of people who don't know who you are. As a general rule, these types of rules are generated by people who want to keep watch and control other people. Intelligent people follow their God, if they are believers obviously, but they do not let themselves be lead by other people who are not God to control them. This takes us to the next point, which is what we should really think of as believers, putting aside other people who believe in the same God as we do.

2.- **I don't think it is something good in the eyes of God**: if according to your belief, God created man and woman just as we are, and as people we enjoy penetration, kisses on the lips and embracement, what would the real reason be for not being able to kiss any part of the body of the person we love? The penis is simply another part of the body, it's not better or worse, it's only another area and equally like the rest likes to be pampered and kissed. A hand is used to hold objects or to work with, however, it doesn't mean it can't be kissed. The reproductive member is used for this purpose, to procreate among other things, but that doesn't mean it can't be kissed or receive pleasure. What's more, if God had not wanted it to be, it would have been made in such a way to create without the other being possible. On the other hand, everyone who enjoys fellatio and cunnilingus in a healthy way see it together with penetration as the closest way to feel the complementarity of the couple. The belief that God created man and woman as complementary couldn't be better expressed than this way.

3.- **It is a disgusting act, dirty or repugnant**: there are
many people who see the sexual organs as dirty areas. If
these areas are kept clean and taken care of, they're simply
another part of the body that just as we mentioned before,
also need love and affection. If it's the taste that we reject
we can always use flavored products such as flavored
lubricants, cream, chocolate syrup, etc. At first it's normal
that this experience doesn't seem very attractive from the
things we've heard since our childhood, however, as we try
out this practice we'll like it more and more as we go along,
especially for the pleasure that our partner feels with it.
Using a flavored condom helps a lot at first as there's no
direct contact and at the same time it's a way to prevent
diseases as mentioned previously. And above all, if there is
already rejection in practicing this, let's try to take him
gently asking him that we'd like to share a moment in the
shower under the falling water together with him and wash
ourselves with care and sensuality (let's not forget to wash
the rest of his body too so he doesn't think that we only
wanted to go there to wash his intimate parts) and kissing

him in the meantime. This way, we'll know for certain that it's clean. We can also choose a bath gel that leaves a pleasant specific smell on the skin, so if we notice, we alone can fix almost all our concerns about it.

4.- **I have no idea, he'll laugh at me and maybe I could hurt him**: if this is our worry, let's not worry. From hereon, we'll see what is to be done and how. We'll become real muses of the art of oral sex.

3

PHYSICAL PARTS TO BEAR IN MIND IN ORAL SEX

"Love is between souls, sex is between bodies".

Anonymous

This chapter is very important to be able to continue to differentiate well some areas from others and therefore understand well and imagine with detail the steps that are given in this manual.

During oral sex, we must not see the penis as the only element. We must know how to differentiate each of its parts to play with and stimuate each one of them. We should keep interchanging our object of stimulation, and keep the man's desire rising and trembling with pleasure.

The jewel of the crown is **the glans**. The top part of the penis, the head, is where the most sensitive part of the penis is. It's the most erogenous area and, therefore, with which we can offer our man the most pleasure. The same way, being such a sensitive part, we must be very careful, because the rubbing of our teeth or too much pressure could result very unpleasant or even do harm.

To stimulate this area, we can cover the glans with our mouth or our lips, and massage it with soft movements. At the same time, if we have the penis in our mouth, we can play with our tongue: licking its glans or giving light taps.

A specific area of the glans is **the frenulum or frenum**. This joins the inner side of the glans with the inner surface of the foreskin (the piece of skin that covers the glans). It's small, it has a triangular shape and it's found opposite of the abdomen (not facing it but on the other side of the penis). This area specifically has many nerve endings, so it is also a very erogenous area. Nevertheless, when circumcision is performed to eliminate the foreskin, many times the frenulum is also eliminated. Even so, and in spite of being less marked, stimulating this area on men can also create great pleasure.

One way of stimulating is to run the tongue from up down and then down up interspersing slowly and gently giving quick touches with the tip of the tongue. We achieve the latter in the following manner: pronounce the syllable "LA" in a continuous way (lalalala) out loud. Increase the speed as much as possible. Once we feel the speed of the tongue and the exact movement, we'll then know exactly how to give quick touches on the frenelum, that is exactly the technique to use (but let's remember to only do it once in a while, because goodness is brief and in small amounts, therefore twice as good; when the good is repeated too much, it ceases to have that special touch and therefore no longer so desired). We can also give it soft and moist kisses with our lips. If we want to give it more intensity, we can give it little taps with the tip of the tongue. A lot of stimulation in that area may produce an ejaculatory reflex prematurely.

Another very important part of the glans is its **crown**. This is the area that covers the whole base of the glans, and in case of foreskin, it's the part that is covered when the member isn't erected. It's the limit that divides the glans from the trunk. As well as the whole glans, this area also provides a lot of pleasure. If we focus our resources on this area, we should use our tongue and run it over the whole surface of the crown, from one side to the other, as if it were an ice cream cone. We can also insert the penis in our mouth until this area is covered, and with our moist lips, put a little pressure on the crown. We can do light movements from up down or, even turning slightly on the base of the glans. This technique allows us to use our tongue on the frenelum or on another part of the glans. The movements that can be done in this area are quite varied: turning the mouth over it making circles with the lips, forming spirals around it with the tongue making circles from down going up and from up going down. Another thing they like very much is forming a small circle with our lips simulating the hole of the vagina when it's not yet stimulated, and then insert the glans gradually, giving the sensation as if it's forcing its way into the entrance through the "hole" that is opening little by little and letting it enter. In this case we must bear in mind our man's sensitivity, because some of them need a lot of lubricating so as not to feel any pain. It's necessary to watch his expression and ask if it hurts or explicitly ask if anything that might hurt even if just a little, to let us know immediately so we can find out the points from which to start off with as far as his needs, tastes and sensitivity to pain are concerned. Another thing that can be done in this area, once the glans is inserted in our mouth, is to pressure with our lips forming a big O and then converting it to a small o, repeating this process alternating slowly and then quickly, using the tongue once in a while to tap the outlet hole of the semen or over the skin of the glans. These techniques can drive him crazy if we keep the pressure and speed in mind, among other things which we'll talk about further on.

Generally, the glans is the area which we should dedicate more time to, however, we shouldn't overdo it, because if we spend too much time doing it, he could reach an orgasm too quickly, and the enjoyment will be over too soon (it could also be in reverse, he could get so tired that later he might not like it so much, let's remember that satiety only leads to eliminating what was enjoyed at the beginning). What's more, for some men too much stimulation given in the glans produces an annoying tingling sensation in them. This is why we should interchange from stimulating the glans to other areas as well.

Anyway, if we notice that the arousement in our man begins to descend, or his member loses firmness, we should resort back to stimulating the glans.

The trunk and base of the penis is also a sector that you should work on. To give the glans a little rest and not succumb to the pleasure its stimulation brings, we can proceed to massage other areas of the penis. If we look, there is a straight line, more or less marked, that goes from the frenulum to the base of the penis. We can run our tongue fully extended along this line, from the base of the penis till we reach the frenulum. Another way of stimulating the trunk is using our lips. We put our head perpendicular to our man's penis and with our mouth open, we put the base of the penis between our lips, as if we'd like to bite it, but of course, without using our teeth. Next, we go up and down with our lips all over the trunk, slightly pressing our lips. This technique is as if we were masterbating with our hands. This form of pleasure is one of the most gentle ones, so it shouldn't be used too quickly, but only as a rest period because if it's used for a long period of time, the man's arousement drops dramatically. Techniques that can be used for a longer period of time in this area are to insert the whole member into the mouth (at least as much as possible, without reaching the throat so as to be able to play around easily), and once inside, play with the tongue making circles around the phallus or running the tongue from down up and from up down, pressing with it in some areas more than others, etc. It's simply a matter of playing a little in that area.

We can even use the hands and resort to them to massage this area (oral sex doesn't have to be done only with the mouth, what's more, using the hands can help us not only to rest but even excite him more by using both). While we stimulate the glans or the upper part of the trunk, we can surround the base of the penis with our fingers and put pressure on it. Press firmly but without overdoing it, we don't want to squeeze the penis. Being that the blood is concentrated in the glans, if we squeeze the base, we don't allow the blood to flow from the penis, thus only achieving it to swell more. This will serve us in occasions when we see the penis beginning to get flaccid. On the other hand, we can also use the hands to circle them around the base of the penis and make up and down movements, or even rotary ones. In these cases, it's convenient to use vaseline or some kind of lubricant, so that the movements are smooth and don't create annoying friction.

If we keep going lower, we'll find the testicles, and more specifically, with the scrotum, which is the skin that covers them. Although the stimulation in this area isn't as pleasant as the glans, we must also be very careful with the practices that are done, as the testicles are very sensitive, any kind of bump could create annoyance and pain in our man.

The stimulation we choose for this area will depend on the state our man has it in. It may be unshaven and could give us qualms to use our mouth with so much hair. So then we can resort to our hands. We can put his testicles in our palm and give a light massage, as if we'd like to catch them with our hand, but as it's already been said, with a lot of care. If our nails are somewhat long, we can also run them across the skin of the scrotum. Some men love this. However, to perform this game, the nails must be very well taken care of, if not, we could hurt it from unpleasant grazing. We must remember to use gentleness and tenderness in this area. What really does drive them crazy is gradually inserting and absorbing softly one of the testicles into our mouth while we moan with pleasure from it making "mmm's" or "grrr's" in a low and guttural sound.

In case you're not shy or the area is shaven, we can move on to another level and use the tongue and lips. We can put one of the testicles in our mouth and gently lick and suck it. If we really look, there is a line that runs through the scrotum and divides in two. This pleat is also very sensitive, so we can run over that entire area at the same time with the whole tongue from down going up, or giving light and soft taps with the tip of the tongue like skipping through a stream over the stones and pebbles.

Another place that requires our attention is **the perineum**. This is the part that is between the scrotum and the anus. By being very near to the prostate, which is the masculine G spot, a proper stimulation can get a man aroused very quickly. What's more, it's recommended to put pressure on it evey now and then, especially when he's just about to finish. This area also may have hair and just like the scrotum, it is up to us to decide if we want to stimulate it and how. We can resort to a simple massage with the fingers, pressing a little and making small circles in the area. Or if we're up to it, we can lick it and give soft kisses around the perineum.

And finally, an area that can also be stimulated is

the anus. This matter is a bit involved, since many men will have it as something forbidden, a taboo matter. But while it's true, the masculine G spot is found in the prostate, and one way of stimulating it is through the anus. However, we will not speak of the masculine G spot stimulation itself, but rather of the aureole of the anus. This area is also very sensitive, and it can be stimulated with soft circular movements with the finger or the tongue. As it was mentioned previously, this area is a bit involved, and not only for men, but for us as well. We may feel repulsion towards the area in question, and bad hygiene on the man's part could be very unpleasant. A very effective and safe alternative would be to use some kind of masculine preservative, a condom. We can make a vertical cut in the condom and extend it over the anal area. This way we can lick it and play around this area all we want without having to worry about our partner's personal hygiene.

The **prostate or P or G spot**, in case it hasn't been clearly specified, is on the inside so it can't be seen in plain sight. The prostate is just behind the perineum, found between the bladder and rectum. This is why its stimulation can be given either pressing on the perineum or in the anal area. How do you get to the G spot through the rectum? It's situated about five centimeters (approximately two and a half inches) from the anus. It's a lump that's about the size of a walnut; putting pressure on it, the man feels a pleasure that has nothing to do with those he can perceive in his genitals. What's more, thanks to its rubbing that this can get our lover to have an ejaculation twice as powerful and produce double the satisfaction. The orgasms are always much more intense and the ejaculations much more potent, thanks to the stimulation of this particular spot. The prostate massage or stimulation used at the same time that our man is penetrating us combines two incredible sensations provoking at the same time a compendium of excitement of a different type making the satisfaction surpass the limits or the man's expectations.

There are men who reject this type of practice thinking that feeling pleasure could mean being gay, especially if the man is homophobic. Society still has to advance quite a bit regarding these topics, in accepting people as they are and not for their needs or their sexual inclination (which by the way, is genetic, and therefore should be accepted exactly the same as the people who are blonds, redheads or brunettes). We want to emphasize the fact that if a man likes to be rubbed in this specific spot (they all like it because it's something normal and logical), has nothing to do with being a heterosexual or homosexual. It's just simply another pleasurable spot. One thing we must have clear is, to look for this spot in our partner, there should be enough implication between both to be able to share without any fears or false beliefs, but on the contrary, looking for mutual satisfaction, as well as the one receiving the delight as the one giving it. If the man is embarrassed or even afraid of getting hurt, the best would be to explain what we're going to do and make it very clear that in the moment he wants to stop, all he has to do is say so, we'll stop and quit the practice.

There are two ways to stimulate the prostate: directly and indirectly. The direct way is introducing the finger or an object for example like a dildo and directly rub the spot inside the anus. Indirectly is achieved by helping us with the penis. We must differentiate the two types of erections that exist: one of the them is when the penis is aroused it goes towards the navel being almost parallel to the stomach, and the other one is erect like aiming straight out front. This process is ONLY produced when the erection is directed towards the navel and is close to it. It's achieved by bringing it closer to the stomach, because with this action it gets the cavernous bodies to open up a little more. We use this method when we're satisfying our man without penetration, of course. The other way to achieve this is pressing on the perineum (where the seam of the pants generally are), which is the area that goes from the testicles to the anus. This area is enormously satisfactory for the man when he's just about to ejaculate. The way to make him enjoy it is, taking the testicles in the hands gently because at this point is when they're most sensititve, and bring them slightly towards the front to stimulate the perineum more easily. Let's be careful with this technique making it gentle and taking great care of the extent to which we bring them towards us by lifting them; moving them just a little so that the skin that goes from the testicles to the perineum tenses a bit. We will be pressing with the thumb making sure to be careful if we have long nails. You should only press with the tip of the finger, because we only want to put pressure on that spot. Pressure can be put on one single spot, we can make circles and even move the finger from up going down, and from down going up running a continuous line with a little more speed as the time approaches when our lover will finish.

A tip to bear in mind is if we're going to stimulate the man directly in his G or P spot (prostate), is to have on hand: lubricants, wet towels and condoms (there are people who use latex gloves but this could reduce the eroticism of the moment due to the coldness that could contribute to being reminded of surgical matters, it would be advisable when and if we're going to play the roll of doctors and nurses). It's also important that the man is previously really stimulated and "hot", relaxed. Another essential point is that, the nail on our index finger which is what we will use in this process, be well trimmed and filed.

Many times, at the moment when we begin to insert our finger into the anus, the man contracts or closes it. In these moments we must avoid pulling the finger out, and just leave it where it is at the same time that we continue to stimulate other areas such as the penis or the perineum gently and sweetly. We must be slow and patient at the time of inserting the finger or dildo (for the first times around it's advisable to use the finger as it's smaller, flexible and more intimate leaving coldness aside). A dildo should only be used if he already feels completely secure about using it. At about two or three centimeters we'll notice a little bump, that exactly is the prostate. This is our man's G spot. Sometimes it can be found at about five centimeters, everything depends on our man. What we can do as we get there: caress it, tap it or simply touch it. We can get to like this spot too much because of how easy it is for him to discharge, sometimes even without stimulation anywhere else.

As previously mentioned with anal stimulation, it's a delicate subject, that's why before we go any further in working on this area, we must know for certain if our partner will like it, so the easiest thing to do is to ask him out openly. The same goes for the rest of the areas. By the general rule, the majority of men like oral sex, but surely each one has some specific preferences as far as intensity, time and areas, etc are concerned.

4

ORAL SEX THROUGH THE EYES

"She is the ornament of her sex".
Charles Dickens

One of the most important senses when it comes to sexual relations are the eyes, and more so when it involves oral sex. It's obvious that the sense of touch and the feelings that are experienced in the stimulation of the penis are essential, but for that, watching how we do it turns them on very much, it makes them feel the fire inside. For all that, we'll explain some of the aspects that we should bear in mind to offer the best visual experience.

First, we must think of what **clothes** we're going to wear. If we want to play with his imagination a little and make him see that we're playful, we can put on a dress that's somewhat transparent or red lingerie. If we want to go a little further and take on a more dominant roll, we can wear some kind of garment that looks like leather, for example. We can leave all this clothing on or take them off little by little, depending how we feel more comfortable and notice the need for it (if he wants to see something more, he'll surely let us know). In the chapter that covers the roles we can play, we'll see each of the different clothing we can use in detail.

A **striptease** before oral sex can also be useful to warm up our man. If we have any idea of the basics in dancing, we can make sensual movements to the rhythm of a slow song, while we're taking off our clothes. It's very important to keep our eye on our partner. This fixed look will make him feel desired and to us it will give information of whether he's liking it or not. This way we can also know how far we can go, he could be satisfied by just seeing our breasts exposed, or maybe prefers it all the way... Once the striptease is over, our guy will be so aroused that we could go ahead and work on his penis without having to do anymore foreplay. Another alternative would be that our man is the one who'll be taking off our clothes, until we're down to our sexy lingerie or, if we like, completely nude.

Another point to keep in mind is the **make-up**. Many women like to dress up so they look more attractive and that isn't a problem either. However, when the time comes to practicing oral sex to a man, it could bring us problems. We must think what kind of lipstick we should use, because we don't want it all over our face. For this we can use a lipstick especially designed so it doesn't come off or leave any lipstick marks. We can also use a shiny gloss that gives a moist feeling to the lips, as this is something that arouses them to a great degree. It's also true that there are men who get aroused when their penis is slightly stained with lipstick. But as explained before, with make-up smeared on our face definitely doesn't look very attractive.

The type of make-up to use goes directly linked to the roll we want to play, of which will be discussed in the chapter dedicated to role play further ahead.

On the other hand, we should never forget our **attitude**. It's very important to know what role we'll be playing in the game and adapt our make-up, our lingerie and our behavior in this role accordingly, just as it's been said before. For instance, if we want to seem hard, firm and dominant, but our attitude says otherwise, no matter how much we wear a leather outfit with a whip, we're not going to inspire any kind of respect. We must believe our role. My queens, don't forget that WE ARE GODDESSES!!! We just have to realize it and use our female powers, powers that each and every one of us have, be what we may be physically or mentally.

Lastly, most important is **to look in the eyes** of our man while we're giving him oral sex. It is true that depending on the position we're in, this will be more or less easy. However, eye contact should be kept whenever possible. We can look at him while we're running our tongue over every part of his penis. It's not simply looking at him every now and then, it's letting him know that we're enjoying this practice, transmitting to him that our greatest desire at that moment is to give him oral sex, that we're melting inside simply for giving him pleasure.

Some men, when they're about to finish, prefer to masterbate themselves to control their orgasm. To help him, we can open our mouth and stick out our tongue in a lecherous way, so that he knows that we want him to finish off inside of us or simply that we love to see him finish off wherever he does it. We can even tell him where we would like him to finish, on our breasts, on our back, in our mouth or wherever we wish. Seeing all this willingness on our part will also arouse him very much.

As a complimentary gesture, we could put on a mask that allows him to see the eyes but with our face half covered. It would be as if someone else would be giving him oral sex. This could be a point to keep in mind at the hour of playing roll games or satisfying some other fantasy. However, this is something that would be done approximately every three months or so, as what we really want is for him to remember every single detail of our face, our body and our mind in the process (the latter meaning the way in which we use it to build up the strategy of how to take the steps to drive him crazy with pleasure and passion).

5

ORAL SEX THROUGH SMELL

"Your scent of earth in heat approaches me and I navigate the body like a boat ".

Jorge Debravo

The scent of the environment and our perfume are also details too important to leave out and it has also been proven that certain aromas give us more sexual arousal to both men and women.

For example, **orange, lavander, vanilla, jasmine, cinnamon, patchouli**... These are aromas that seem to increase sexual desire. Therefore, we can make use of some of these scents to increase the desire during our sexual relations.

First, it would be good to take a relaxing shower. We can use a **shampoo or gel** with some of the scents suggested above (or any other one that we know of that our man really likes) so that our body and hair gives off an irresistable smell. If possible, we should choose a shampoo and body gel with the same scent, otherwise two different scents mixed together might not be so ideal.

Secondly, we can use some of the scents already suggested to perfume the air with an **aromatic candle** or with **incense**. In the same way as the other, let's make sure the scent of our body is compatible with the room.

When we're already in the middle of the action, we could resort to a bit of **chocolate** syrup. The smell of cocoa also increases the excitement and if we use it to spread on our man's penis as well, we can use the excuse to play a fun game.

Lastly, we must be aware of the role we're going to play during our sex session and adapt the aromas to the scene. For example, if we're going to play a submissive, passive and calm role, we should use sweeter type aromas; or instead, if our role is going to be more of a warrior, dominant and active type, we should resort to fresher aromas, the opposite to what is usually thought.

If a word could be chosen to give the scent of love a name, it would be: pheromones. If we've never heard of them, this may be the moment to inquire about it. Pheromones are chemical substances that we release (body smell) and makes the other person desire us more. Androstenol causes the man to get aroused and androsterone gets the woman to feel the need to join the man in a sexual act. There's a big world of different products for the intimate moment related to these substances. It is not recommended to use them carelessly, but to use them only occasionally. The most common way is using massage oils to tone up the person who's receiving it.

The fact of giving him a massage before oral sex can make us more receptive as far as making him enjoy it goes. However, if in case we feel very stressed about making him enjoy it this way because it's one of our first times or we feel embarrassed or we don't feel prepared, we can ask him to give us the massage with the pheromone oils; this way we relax at the same time that we get aroused and we'll be more willing to go ahead with it.

Finally, and not because it's any less important, we already talked about the man's hygiene but we must not forget ours as well. You need to be clean and trim not only to receive but also to give. The scent of perfume should not be used to cover up any odors, but to give a touch of some scented note on our clean skin. Our pheromones will come out by themselves from the moment we start to get aroused, and so for these to produce a positive effect, they need to differ from the smell body sweat can bring on even before the relation in itself.

6

ORAL SEX THROUGH TOUCH

"Lovers know very well that there are caresses that are not just a mere caress but a possession".

José Angel Buesa

Regarding touch, the first aspect that we must be aware of is the softness of **our skin**. Men love to feel our skin fine and smooth. For this, it wouldn't hurt us to use a moisterizing cream to take care of our body. What's more, if it's scented like some of the aromas mentioned earlier, much better still, although in case the cream has a rather noticeable scent, we should choose not to use any perfume and use the cream instead. There are moisterizing creams that have specific scents and there is a large variety to choose from.

On the other hand, it is also convenient we take care o f **our hair**. Besides a good shampoo, it would also be appropriate to use some kind of creme rinse. Men like to run their fingers through our hair while we're giving them oral sex, so it's also recommended to wear your hair down, so that they can run their fingers through our hair freely.

In regard ot our **lingerie**, we should know that the touch of silk is very pleasant. In addition, it gives an air of sofistication that can play a point in our favor at the moment of increasing our man's desire. That's why, if we want to put the cherry on the cake, we can also use satin sheets on our bed.

If we want to give it a more daring and warrior touch, we can go on to leather-like clothes. Besides a visual aspect, touch can result more erotic and shows our weapons, we can show him that tonight we are the ones in charge. On the contrary, if we pretend to be more subtle, we can resort to lacy lingerie or net type stockings. This detail provides a playful and naughty point at night, but without us having to take the lead.

Lastly, we should also be aware of the position in which we give oral sex. It would be convenient for our man to have full access to all parts of our body. This way, while we stimulate orally, he can caress our **breasts**, touch our **buttocks,** or stimulate the clitoris. All this, besides producing us pleasure, it will also arouse our man. On the other hand, we can decide that he can't touch us or himself if we don't give him permission to do so.

Now, we'll mention a point too important to ignore. It's about the pressure and the speed we use with our hands or other parts of our body on his body. Other ways to feel skin to skin is with our lips, tongue, breasts, etc.

We can use the lips sweetly over his pectorals, his

arms, his lips, his neck, his abdomen and of course, his thighs preferably doing it from the knees towards his member interchanging the frontal area with the inner area and as we get closer to the central point we focus only on the inner areas of his legs. This arouses them in a fast and impressive way seeing us going towards a point so important such as his genitals. We can alternate with the tongue going up gradually.

We can use the tongue in a special way on the neck running it from the bottom of his chin or from the shoulder making a soft and slow circuit towards the back of one of his ears, especially his left side which is the most sensitive part of the body (this is because if he's right handed, the right side would be more adapted to everything; if on the contrary he's left handed, the area to choose would be the right side).

We can brush our breast over his chest or over the back when we're giving him a massage. We can also start from below going up towards his lips to kiss him passing from the abdominal area going upwards brushing with the breast from his intimate parts till his pectorals.

Two of the most important things that make a difference between normal oral sex and the one that leaves a mark forever are pressure and speed. Although these could be discussed in this subject-matter, we'll dedicate a special space for this in the last subject of the manual.

Once we've seen the parts that we can use, we'll go on to external things we can use:

Fizzy type candies: this causes a great sensation on our partner's member especially   for being a new sensation never felt before. The best way to use them is to put a little in our mouth so it mixes with our saliva, and then immediately put the member in our mouth.

Cream: using whipped cream like what we use on strawberries can be very amusing, from massaging ourselves with it on our breasts to then spreading it completely on his member and even on his scrotum to lick it up afterwards, or even spreading it directly on him (we can also use ice cream as an alternative). Something they may like a great deal is asking them to spread the cream themselves making a trail for us to follow with the tongue or absorbing it with our lips; but of course, under one condition: that they spread it everywhere except on his member, leaving that part for when we decide. Let's not forget to keep hold of the reins, independently of the role we're playing.

Ice: it can be used at precise moments such as sliding it over our intimate parts in front of him including the nipples and this way arouse him within his sight while we continue satisfying him in oral sex, also directly on his member so he notices the difference between the cold from the ice and the warmth from the inside of our mouth. We can also put a small or medium sized piece of ice in our mouth to play with him while his member is inside of our mouth.

Hot candle wax: we must be careful with wax because not all men accept it depending on their sensitivity. If he does like it you have to observe how much, we must remember that the skin of the penis is very sensitive and what we least want is to change the pleasure of oral sex to pain. It's better to ask before anything and try it out on a day when we're not doing any oral sex; which means to say, that when we're going to do it, we want to be very clear where the limits are.

Wine: this drink or any other like sangria can be tremendously exciting helping to disinhibit ourselves to do oral sex on our partner. He can make trails with the wine on his skin and then we follow it savoring it with our tongue.

Chocolate: we can use syrup, the kind that comes already prepared in the stores or warmed up chocolates (just when they start to melt) and make drawings on his body directly with the tongue or with the finger and then lick it up.

7

ORAL SEX THROUGH SOUND

"Words are the most powerful drug used by mankind".
Rudyard Kipling

To express with moans and words what one feels makes the pleasure much more powerful. So, the question is how to take advantage of it?

It was previously mentioned that we should make our man see that we enjoy practicing oral sex. One way of doing it is through **moans**. If we show him our satisfaction, our desire to make him enjoy it, we'll see how his arousement increases and he twists and turns with pleasure.

Another thing that also heats up many men is the sound of **slight heaves or gags** while we have his entire penis in our throat. Knowing that their penis almost chokes us, makes them feel much more manly, their ego increases and makes them feel like they have the largest penis in the world. However, we must be careful, because if we get carried away with this technique, we could have an unpleasant surprise, since vomiting is pretty anti-erotic. Besides, we ourselves might not like the sound of it or its effect, so if that's the case, might as well just leave it all together, as it isn't something necessary for oral sex to be satisfactory. What's more, it's not one of the main points to consider in order to make the best of oral sex, it's only a question of some men liking it and others who don't.

On the other hand, there are two ways that you can turn to in arousing a man through words:

First, we can be the ones to take the lead. We can take on the **role of the queen** and be the ones who decide what to do the whole time. We'll make our man beg us for a little bit of pleasure. We can ask questions such as: "Who is your queen?", "Who is your goddess?", "What is the best thing that has ever happened in your life?", etc. If he answers what we want to hear, we can stimulate the area that arouses him most, or take his hands and place them on our breasts. Instead, if we want to make him suffer a little, we can pretend that we're going to lick the penis but only stay near it, without doing it. These pauses will increase his longing and his arousal. Depending on the dominance level we want to exercise, instead of asking us what he wants us to do to him, we can demand him to beg for it, and we be the ones to decide whether we'll give it to him or not. Lastly, when he's about to reach his orgasm, we can demand him to repeat our name, this will make him always remember who the queen is that gives him so much pleasure.

Second, **the role of God** we would give to our man. He'd be the one to demand which is the area he wants for us to stimulate and how and we would satisfy each and every one of his wishes. We must make him notice that we are at his service, that giving him pleasure is our greatest desire, that he is our man and is the best in the world.

We must be very careful with these kind of games and try not to go over the limit, since some men get aroused by saying dirty things while they're having sexual relations. We must be consistent and, if we don't like him calling us "slut" or saying dirty things, we must let him know before we begin so we don't feel hurt afterwards. We must equally remember that in sex the role play and illusions or mental scenes have very little or nothing to do with the life outside of it. We can suggest for him to call us by our name, even though later in his mind he'll be imagining some dirty things in case we don't want to hear them. Nevertheless, if we don't have a problem with our man adopting this type of role, we can play along with the role and use phrases such as: "It's so big!" or "I love to suck it". Let's allow our imagination to fly high and make his enjoyment that much greater.

Moans, say dirty things, make noise with the tongue and saliva, is the best way to make us notice and make our man see that we're enjoying the sex session very much. (In the courses and the specific book on moans and what to say in bed, you can see the types that exist in a variety of details, how to use them and when, as well as the words and phrases to use).

8

ORAL SEX THROUGH TASTE

"To love can be a bitter taste in the mouth, but it is worth it if in the end the sweetness of your lips reward your bitterness".

Anonymous

Considering that we are the ones using our mouth and our tongue to perform oral sex, this section is addressed to us more than to our men.

In the first place, just like it's been mentioned in a previous chapter, there is one point to be very aware of and that is **cleanliness** in the intimate masculine area. If we don't think that there is sufficient hygiene for us to put our mouth in that area we must let him know. It's very important that we don't force the issue or show disgust, because he'll notice it. But in the same way, we won't tell him abruptly either, because we could hurt our partner's pride. We must know how to say it. One possible solution would be to do foreplay in the shower. Start kissing under the water and soaping each of his parts, and then go on to massaging the pectorals, abdomen, buttocks, his muscles and finally his genitals. In the same way, he can also be soaping every part of our body. Once we're finished showering, we can procede to give way to our imagination, without worrying about unpleasant odors. With this technique, we'll have achieved to have his penis freshly washed and it will serve as foreplay as well.

In regard to oral sex itself, we can turn to different flavors to play with. For example, **cream, chocolate, caramel syrup, jam or marmelade, fruit, gum drops,**

flavored gels, etc. We can spread a little cream or chocolate over his glans, then go on to licking and sucking it until there's nothing left. Our man will enjoy a good stimulation and we will relish it. Or we can also spread fruit and gum drops around the base of his penis and eat them while we kiss the area. However, using external foods or flavored products, can also be good in case it's the first time we're doing it, but as we keep repeating and if we really like our partner and we really feel attracted to it, we'll surely like it's own taste itself. Yes, we're referring to the taste of his skin, which usually is a mixture of sweet and salty, depending on the person (some skins taste sweeter and others more salty).

Lastly, one issue that should also be considered in this section is the **taste of the semen**. Although we don't want to swallow it, many men get aroused by finishing off in our mouth, and whether we like it or not, we end up savoring its taste. There are times when the taste is pretty unpleasant, so we can turn to chewing a piece of gum or eat a piece of candy.

We can also try for the liquid to stay on the sides of

the tongue or underneath it so it touches our taste buds as little as possible, which is where we perceive the taste of things. So, avoid contact with the semen by lifting the top part of the tongue as much as possible to its full extent. Once this is done, showing a smile without opening the mouth, we can go straight to the bathroom or use a tissue to spit it out with discretion, and form a ball with the tissue so the liquid doesn't spill and so our partner doesn't have to see that we spat it out.

This way, we don't swallow it and we won't feel the taste (at least not completely). However, there are other techniques to counteract the savor and change its taste. Further on, in another section, it'll be discussed more closely.

9

ORAL SEX THROUGH FEELINGS

"The beauty of a sexual relationship is in the spontaneity of the conquest and the secret in which that conquest is made".

Reinaldo Arenas

Once having already discussed each of the five senses, it's necessary to cover the matter of feelings in more detail, which would be a specific aspect of touch, and although we've slightly already covered the subject, let's take another look in this chapter separately. During oral sex, play with caresses, touches, kisses, the temperature... The use of these will make you live the experience with greater intensity.

First, we can turn to **our hands**. Our hands can be the perfect complement at the time of performing oral sex. For example, we can caress and massage the testicles with one hand, while with the other lightly masterbate the base of the penis, and with our mouth stimulate his glans. Another possibility is with circular movements softly press his perineum; this way, we'll notice how his erection increases considerably. When we use our hands in oral sex, it is absolutely advisable to use lubricant to avoid too much friction. We can make ascending and descending movements, or go slightly rotating our wrist along the length and width of his penis. If we're more rebellious, we can give little taps, but we must be careful where we give them and the degree of acceptance of this practice by our lover. We can play with his buttocks, his thighs, even with the base of his penis, but we must be very careful with the testicles and the glans. We can also turn to pinching, but the same areas must be taken into consideration, avoiding some of the areas such as the penis and the testicles; which means pinching are only advisable in other areas that don't interfere with the genitals. Finally, as has been mentioned in a previous section, some men like it when you graze the nails over the scrotum, but it must be done very carefully, despite that the game is pretty much recommended.

As always remember, here are some suggested general ideas that do not have to be the ones that your guy likes. This is why we must be observative and watch his gestures or looks to see what he likes or not in order to capture his tastes and limits. And if we have any questions, we shouldn't hesitate to ask him.

Secondly, we have the **lips**. We can start by approaching our moist lips to his glans, and with the mouth closed, rub his penis over our lips as if it were lipstick. Then gradually, we open our mouth until forming an "O" shape and slip the lips downwards until we cover his glans completely. At this point, if we press a little with our lips, we can emulate the feeling of penetrating a virgin girl, as we've already mentioned in another chapter. At the same time, we can lick his frenulum a little with the tongue or give it light taps. If we want to go a little further, we can continue inserting the penis as far as we can, and following the routine of going up and down. To add a little stimulation, we can swirve the mouth as we go up and down. We can also give little kisses along his penis and the scrotum. Finally, we can alternate it with small suctions while we're giving kisses. Gentle breathing all along his penis and his scrotum would also be very welcome.

Thirdly, we have the **tongue**. Although these techniques may seem less stimulating than using the mouth, it can produce a great satisfaction if used appropriately, and may even like it more. In addition, it's handy for resting our mouth a little and change positions.

We can start by licking the perineum, pressing with the tongue extended, or giving light touches with the tip of the tongue. Then we go to the scrotum. Here we should be more careful, we can lick his testicles as if they were a ball of ice-cream. Gradually, we can go up till the base of his penis, where we will be licking with the tongue extended, from down going up. Lastly, we get to the glans. In this area is where we should play more. We can stimulate the frenulum with the tongue extended (very important; although we can give small and quick taps with the tongue in this area, one big lick or several ones arouses them very much), as if it were a lollipop with some spunk in it. For some men this might cause them to ejaculate very soon. We can also go on to licking the crown of the glans. Here we should use the tip of the tongue and run along the entire surface, but without a lot of pressure, just brushing it making it feel like a feather perched discontinuously. Finally, we can play with the glans in general, lick the entire area with an extended tongue, alternating fast and slow movements; or give little taps with the tip of the tongue.

And lastly there is the **mouth**. With it we can use the suction technique, which is one of the most important in the art of oral sex; it is what will provide our guy with the greatest pleasure.

The suction technique is the most important of them

all, it is the excellence of oral sex and this is becau.

nothing else nor any part of our body that provokes such a

feeling. It consists in producing a feeling of emptiness, and this act goes from light suction with the mouth to complete absorption. It's about sucking or absorbing. We can try with a banana, close our lips over it and we suck its tip inwards absorbing the air inwards, although in this case it's not the air that really comes in, it's the banana. If we've tried with one of these before, we'll see then that it's much more pleasant doing it with our partner's member and it's something very satisfactory for the one who receives as for the one who gives it. It can be used in any area, however, the two most recommended are the scrotum and the penis. If we play with the scrotum, we can insert one testicle into the mouth very gradually and then let it out, while we're sucking mildly. Which means to say that, we have two ways to play with suction in this sense: one of them is to open the mouth as much as possible to insert one of the testicles into the mouth and once it's inside, close the mouth so it comes out gradually with out the help of the hands and even making small suctions by re-inserting it a little and letting it out at intervals (starting with everything inside, move the head back to bring out half of the testicle and re-insert a part of what was left outside, move the head back again and suck again the one part that's come out, until the entire testicle is out). Another way is doing it in reverse, start sucking from the skin and gradually absorb the testicle until it's completely inside (it can be done with small absorptions and then a little more or absorbing the entire testicle all at once, smoothly but decisively). Later, using both we can do multiple variations with speed, how much we insert and how much we take out, etc. Let's not forget to do it very carefully and bearing in mind our lover's sensitivity. Once we've finished stimulating this area, we can go on to the base of the penis. We can put our head vertically to the penis and suck on the base, and gradually, go up and then down along the penis. When we get to the glans, we can stimulate it by inserting it completely into our mouth without leaving the frenulum out. Once everything is inside, we can do suctions going upwards, faster or slower, at the same time that we're licking the frenulum. If we want to take it one step further, we can insert the penis into our mouth as far as we can and suck from there till the tip of the penis (from down going up, and from up going down).

As we've seen, there are a lot of techniques and several places where they can be applied. It's important to use the variations and combine them in different ways; each man is a new world to explore, you must experiment to know what he really likes.

Up until now we've been seeing the different elements that can be added to our games, to provide new and intense sensations, some of which have already been mentioned previously.

The first to comment is the **ice**. If we place it directly on the glans, it could be painful, that's why it's preferable that we put a piece of ice on our tongue and move it around in our mouth. Once it's melted, at least most of it, we can start with oral sex. We should especially focus on stimulating the glans which will be the most contrasting thing he can feel, however, we can try on other areas as well. As far as the glans goes, we can run our tongue over the frenulum, the crown or over the glans in general. As our mouth will be cold, we can insert it, and meanwhile, our lips can lightly press on the crown and the tongue can be licking his frenulum. Another alternative to ice that can be used is **ice-cream**. This way, in addition to cooling our tongue, we also introduce the sweet taste of it.

All this contrast between the cold of our mouth and the warmth of his penis will create a feeling that will make him twist and turn with pleasure. In the same way, we can also turn to **warm or cold gels** made especially for sexual activity that produces such a feeling of contrasts as previously described.

However, if we feel that the cold sensation could be a little excessive for our partner, we can try **mint candy**. The fresh feeling will be almost the same and maybe for some of the men who are very sensitive, this would be a better option.

On the opposite side of cold, we have warmth. We can have a **hot drink** before we start oral sex, this way the warmth of our mouth sums up with the excitement of the moment. The same as with the ice, we can play with the glans or experiment with other areas and other techniques used can be the same ones as before: use the tongue over the entire glans, or also add the lips and mouth.

Another way to play with the sensation of warmth is to use **caramel syrup** or chocolate slightly warmed up (attention to "slightly"!!). We can pour it over the scrotum, the penis or the glans and start licking and sucking it up until nothing is left. When applying heat, the blood concentrates in that area, making it more sensitive, and making the sensations much more intense.

If we don't want to use liquids or substances that later may be pretty messy to clean up, we can use a **hot towel**. We can take a piece of cloth and warm it up in the microwave. Then we can spread it over our man's penis and the rest of the erogenous areas, so he notices the higher temperature (by saying higher we don't mean to say hot, because it should really be warm enough to feel pleasant without any exaltations or pain). We can also surround the base of the penis with it and move it up and down, masterbating him.

Finally, if we want to give it a playful and fun touch to our sex session, we can try with some **fizzy candy**. We can put it on the tongue and run it over the glans. Or if we want a little more intensity, put the fizzy candy directly into our mouth and insert the entire glans. The little bursts of the fizzy candy will be felt in the entire area and our man for sure won't be able to stop twisting and turning with pleasure. If the fizzy candy seems too much for us, we can use a **fizzy soda** instead. To do this we put some of the refreshment into our mouth and then introduce the glans. All those bubbles will give a very pleasant tickling sensation to our man.

10

HOW TO PLAY WITH A MAN'S MENTALITY ACCORDING TO OUR PHYSICAL BODY

"You will be the perfect lover when you have sex with the body the same way you do it with the mind, this requires learning because naturally it is much more difficult to govern your fantasies than your body".
Paloma Cobollo

We women must follow some pretty tough beauty

ideals: we must look beautiful, well dressed, wear proper make-up, legs shaven, have a great body, etc. With all these demands, it's normal that the majority of women don't meet up to some ---or various--- of these requirements. It builds a lack of confidence and insecurity in us that influences our behavior, and above all, in our relations with the opposite sex. We should bear in mind and never forget that it is in the differences where the real beauty lies. If we were all the same, all the memories would be too. That is where the magic comes in, in being so different from the rest that we infinitely leave a mark or a print in our partner. It is the difference, our major characteristic and benefit in this game called love.

Although it sounds very idyllic and utopian, we should **accept ourselves** just as we are. Each one of us is different from the rest, and that's what makes us unique and unrepeatable. For as many "imperfections" we may think we have, there's always someone who knows how to see in us all that we are worthy of and our best points. There are always those that in spite of not being especially good looking "attract" a lot, and once you know them, they captivate and trap you. All that is because of their personality and their attitude; and that is what they call "being attractive". That is the most important thing, if we are self confident, we will get much more satisfying relationships.

One way to counteract the negative effects our complexes can have, is to highlight our **strong points**. Maybe we have wide hips that we don't like, but at the same time, maybe we have long legs ---something men just love---; if this is so, we should try to display this quality and leave out what we don't like. There's always something that we can be proud of and want to highlight it.

On the other hand, we can also revert the negative effect of our flaws and convert them into positive points in our favor. Which means, we can take our peculiarities and use them as a part of a **fantasy**. For example, many of us women feel self-conscious about having small breasts. If this is one of the things we feel, we can adopt the role of a young girl, one who's breasts haven't completely developed yet, and who's going to have her first sexual relationship in full puberty. The fantasy of having sex with a virgin is a very recurrent desire among men. But we should be very clear on the fact that we have NO flaws even though we've expressed it in such a way before so as to quickly capture the essence. We're perfect, it's our differences that make us unique. We can do the same with the rest of singularities that we have and which we don't feel completely at ease with or which we feel embarrassed about. All we need is imagination and to know how to play with our partner's fantasies. We can also play the role of someone famous with which we have similar physical features. To have sex with someone famous is another fantasy very common in men.

Short legs: The game with short skirts that start at the waist is a good way to start taking advantage of our legs. If we add a nice pair of high heeled shoes (of a height we can easily and safely walk in) all the better.

Wide hips: generally men love curves, so this particularity shouldn't really be seen as a flaw or something we should be embarrassed about but quite the opposite. Nevertheless, if we want to cover up a little, we can avoid ruffles or tight clothes. The advisable thing is that the garments feel like a second skin. Dark tones stylize the figure. The most appealing colors are divided into three groups, namely, the neutral combining tones of taupe and gray, mystic tones such as garnet / maroon or emerald green, and prints shouldn't be too loud in color (gaudy or too flashy). This doesn't mean we can't use any color or any type of clothing; we're only pointing out some tips that could be useful when we want to camouflage our hips a little.

Small breasts: we have an unlimited variety of different lingerie. In our case we can use the famous "super bra" or "push up" bra to give the breasts more volume at the beginning of the act of being with our lover, but let's not forget that we're beautiful just as we are. With this we're just simply adding to the theme of the erotic game, to warming up and to feel more self confident to begin with. A lot of us women seem to forget quite often how important the neckline shape is and how it creates enormous differences in the perception of our breast, both on our part as well as our partner's. In our case, we can forget about the sports brassiers without padding (choose them only when we're going to do sports knowing that even for these there are brassiers that have underwires and some comfortable filling for this purpose). On the other hand, there's no reason why we should leave comfort out; we can purchase comfortable bras with the option of accommodating some extra padding whenever we wish to do so. For small breasts, the excellent bras are those that have some lace on them or that are completely made of lace. They're elegant, eye-catching and highlight the beauty of the breasts while at the same time create a certain mysticism about them.

Big breasts: if we happen to want to conceal them a little in the beginning, we can wear blouses that have a V-shaped neckline without the cleavage showing and preferably dark tones like black silk or satin; we can wear a blouse with nothing underneath together with a G-string or eye-catching panties. Transparencies can give us a lot of play. Men adore semi-transparencies, net-type stockings, etc. The most recommendable bras are those with underwires that enhance the breasts and semi-transparent without any padding. The finer the fabric, the better. Green and pink tones are usually favorable, and of course, the famous black transparency (which will always be the most sensual and sofisticated). To look more youthful and graceful, if we feel that black is too stern for us, we can look for bras that besides being semi-transparent black or brown full cup or just partially, they could have some kind of design or print around the underwire area. There are bras that form lines on the underwires with silk or satin highlighting in light tones over the darkness of the rest. There are also bras designed especially for women with big breasts, it covers a bit more than half of the breast leaving part of them exposed. It gives the impression that the upper part of the fabric from the cup has been removed, leaving just the seams. That is, leaving the upper part of the breast exposed but continues to form the shape of the bra through the upper seam or wire.

Scars: scars shouldn't be anything to hide, on the contrary, quite the opposite. For men they're signs of pride, that show strength and struggle of survival. All scars have a story behind them and therefore very fascinating and even sexually attractive. If the story behind it is very intimate, we don't have to tell it, in fact we could even use it to magnify its importance. There is nothing more appealing to a man than mysticism and curiosity. We can tell him that the scar is from a very important moment in our lives and we don't want to talk about it, but to be careful not to rub against it too much. This will make him pay more attention and it'll be a point to remember about our person. Scars are a part of our personality, of our journey through life, they are the keys to enter into our deepest memories. That is why we shouldn't only not be embarrassed about them but quite the opposite, we should be proud of them, be where they may be or whatever shape they may have.

Cellulitis: to camouflage it we can use skirts and to eliminate it there are creams especially for that. Sunbathing is one of the things that helps the most, because it's noticed less when tanned.

Overweight: In regard to being overweight there are only two ways to attack it from being ashamed; one is we forget about the standards and enjoy our curves just as they are, helping ourselves if we want, to clothes that give us style according to shapes and tones. The second option is to aim on losing weight in a balanced, healthy way. For that it's advisable to see a specialist who will reinforce the willpower and control (in addition to self esteem), and give us the appropriate advice regarding the number of meals, nutrition, habits, etc. If losing weight is what we really want, let's set our goal. Let's remember that when we feel bad about ourselves, it's not because of the way others see us, but because we don't like ourselves. For this very reason there are only those two solutions: to begin liking ourselves just as we are or strive for our desires and this way feel better about ourselves both inside as out. And of course, while we're on one path or the other, we shouldn't forget that we can enjoy any type of clothing. The good thing about sharing intimate moments is in feeling good with ourselves and enjoying everything we have to give and receive.

Thinness: Using ruffled or frilled lingerie can make us feel more confident due to the game and voluptuousness that this can create. We can play at being a sensitive girl, who needs to be cared for and with the need to satisfy someone to be cared for. On the other hand, being thin has a great point in its favor, and that is, we can use any eye-catching color we want. It is advisable to use light colors to highlight as much as possible.

* Of course, these are just examples and each one of us should know what our limits are and what games we want to create combining the tastes of oneself and those of the man.

SPECIAL STEPS FOR WHEN FEELING ASHAMED:
Things that can help if we feel ashamed:

1.- **Sexy lingerie**:
→ with all kinds of features: from lingerie with precious details such as sequence, lace, embroidery, etc.
→ shapes and colors: bright colors, lively, wild, printed, transparent, net, etc.
→ types of garments: babydolls, corsets, sets, costumes, half body suits, full body suits, skirts, short dresses, bodices, nightgowns, tops, etc.
→ types of fabric: imitation leather, silk, satin, etc.
→ accessories: pendants, earrings, hip pendants, gloves, stockings, pantyhose, suspenders and garters, masks, nipple

covers, bright adhesive linchpins, body decorators, etc.

2.- **Count on a detail** that links to what we are ashamed of with an achievement or success. We've already spoken of this before in the section of scars, and it can be used in almost any range or aspect.

3.- **Exercise**: this isn't only good for our health in itself, but it also helps us release the hormones of happiness called serotonin, dopamine and endorphins. Serotonin gives us a feeling of calmness and helps to reconcile sleep very well, helping us to rest well and feel better (the body recovers in a better way); dopamine gives us a pleasant feeling and helps us reduce the consumption of tobacco or other drugs and sweets. Endorphins on the other hand are the ones that make us feel joy, happiness and even euphoria; it frees us from stress and anxiety. The conclusion we're coming to is that, if we exercise we feel better with ourselves and then when we have sex with our partner, we feel more confident with ourselves and that means leaving shame behind and choose enjoyment in exchange for the absence of it. Feel free to inquire about this subject in the specific manual on the type of exercise especially designed for having awesome sex.

4.- **Drink water**: hydration is essential for our body and that is especially noticeable on the skin. A person who moisterizes their skin regularily keeps it soft, smooth and elastic. It is advisable to drink at least four glasses of water a day. Moisterizing is essential when it comes to doing oral sex, because the more moisterized our skin is, the more oxygen our blood has and that turns into energy, strength of conviction and mental focus in all the steps we want to follow.

5.- **Eat healthy**: nutrition also goes hand in hand with good body maintenance. This way we have strength and resistence when having sexual relations. This is most noticeable at times like when "riding a man", the position in which we are on top of them and doing oral sex.

6.- **Eliminate the darkness progressively**: a lot of us women look for darkness to have sex and the less light there is, the better we feel. For us to get accustomed to the light and feel good in it, there are two things we can do; one is to just do it. For that we can decide to spend an hour with our partner in plain daylight and if possible early in the morning as it is when we are most sensitive regarding this. We can ask for that time so that there is a purely physical recognition of each of the parts of his body and of our own for its part. Once he completely sees all of our "imperfections" and all that we're embarrassed about, we'll feel better when we see that there's nothing to worry about. The other way is to gradually increase the light. We can begin by increasing the number of candles, each time bringing them a bit closer (being careful where we put them so as to obviously avoid any incidents). Then we can turn the light on from a table lamp and then later the ceiling light of the room. Little by little we'll try using natural light more and more until we've accomplished to do any kind of movement and be completely nude in plain daylight.

7.- **Concentration**: letting ourselves go along with the experience and feelings is one of the best things we can do to dismiss any embarrassment we might feel. It's about enjoyment, not about having thoughts in our mind that prevent it. Sex is one of the greatest wonders that we can experience, so all that is opposed to it we must avoid. It's something natural in all human beings and we have the right to enjoy it, both receiving it as giving the best of ourselves for the pleasure of our partner. To be able to focus we must be able to stop irrelevant thoughts. One of the ways is to try to briefly follow a series of steps in oral sex and try not to forget any of them; this way we keep our mind concentrated. One technique that we can use to stop thoughts that don't help us is, we can say STOP! As if we were screaming, but only in our minds, without anyone hearing us. This is interrupting one thought with another, it is often used with quite a bit of diligence in almost all therapies when you want to stop useless thoughts or thoughts that interfere with other tasks, such as for example when you're studying and the mind wanders off to other things that have nothing to do with what you're doing at the moment. It would be of great help to us as we use it more, the easier it will be for us to stop thoughts that we don't want to have and even these will diminish by themselves. The ones we must avoid, just as we've mentioned already, are those such as "I hope he won't see that part of my body", "I hope he doesn't notice my cellulitis", "I don't know what he'll think when he sees my breasts", "it's just that I'm so fat", "and if he thinks I'm too skinny", "and if he doesn't like the way I do it", "and if I hurt him", etc. Let's avoid all this and LET'S ENJOY, which is all that should really matter to us.

8.- **Special games**: one of the games that the psychologists recommend when one of the two partners feels too embarrassed or doesn't enjoy sex like they should is, to spend between one to three days just touching and feeling each other. It works as follows (this would be done if we have enough confidence with our lover): on the first day it's all right to touch any part of the body except the genitals and the breasts. It is true that warming up can become excessive and feel the need to proceed, but we recommend to use mental strength and stop. You can only touch yourselves in those areas and as long as one doesn't touch the other. On the second day you can lightly brush these areas but only in the end; meaning, having already spent some considerable time sharing caresses throughout the rest of the body. On the third day you may already touch and feel more intimately and eventually do oral sex or receive cunnilingus (oral sex on the woman) or have sexual relations directly with intercourse.

9.- **What we think about our body isn't the same as what he thinks**: we people generally have a tendency to self-criticize ourselves: We are taught since childhood that we must be humble and disregard narcissism and self-praise. While it is true that narcissism is not a good way in life, self-praise doesn't necessarily have to be bad, but quite the opposite, it helps us improve our self-esteem. Having it in its proper measure is essential for us to feel good about ourselves. In almost all of the researches where both people in couples have been asked to describe themselves and then describe the other there is a huge difference in how they see themselves and how they see their partner. The descriptions tend to be so different that it's almost unreal. We have a tendency to see ourselves as less attractive and with many more flaws than the way our partner sees us. So, it's essential that we bear in mind when we are with our man, he certainly doesn't see what we consider flaws as such.

10.- **Improve self-esteem**: as we've already mentioned, at the time of having sexual relations of any type it's essential to have a high self-esteem, because if not, we may get unwanted thoughts that could keep us from enjoying everything we could enjoy. In the case that we need to raise our self-esteem, we can get books specialized in this subject, take a course or why not, go and see a psychologist once a week or every two weeks. Going to a psychologist isn't what was thought in previous generations. In New York whoever doesn't see a psychologist is seen as a strange person in the eyes of others. Psychologists don't only help children or people with psychological problems. The majority of patients that go to them are people like us who simply want to learn techniques to improve their day to day schedules as much as in the improvement that supposedly has strategies to overcome the daily problems in a fast, easy and light way to raise self-esteem as we say, and many more other things dealing with everyday life.

11

DIFFERENT ROLES

"In all erotic encounters there is an invisble character and always active: the imagination".

Octavio Paz

Just as it's been said before, during oral sex ----the same as in any other sexual relation— one can adopt a dominant role as well as a submissive one. We will see examples as follows, of the two roles and we'll see what games we can use in each one of them.

On one hand, we can adopt the **active and dominant role**, being us taking charge. With this role, we can play being the boss, nurse, doctor, professor, police, etc. (or simply directing the situation without being anyone but ourselves). During the game, we decide what is to be done, where to stimulate him and in what way. If he squints or complains (without causing him any pain, of course), we can give him a light slap on his penis or on some other part of his body (the area we definitely must avoid on this occasion are the testicles). This act, coming by surprise, will arouse him knowing that this time (in this game) it depends completely on us. We should play with what we know arouses him the most. For instance, if we know that he loves it when we softly lick his frenulum, we can give him a nice lick at first and watch how he twists and turns. Then, we get closer as if we were going to continue but we won't do it, and we can ask him: "do you want more?" and he has to be the one to beg for more.

In the same way, depending on the role we're

playing, we can introduce other games. For example, if we're cops, we can tie his hands or handcuff him to one side of the bed, so his mobility is reduced (like deeper practices such as sadomasochism, bondage, etc., in the manual, "SEX: The magic of BDSM" is explained in greater detail). This deprivation of freedom and knowing that he's completely at our mercy,will arouse him very much. Another example is, if we follow the role of being professors, we can ask questions, such as: Capital of France? And if his answer is correct, we stimulate an area that he likes; and if his answer is wrong, we punish him with a light tap on his member. Perhaps he'll surprise us and give more wrong answers than we imagined, and that point of pain in sex can also be very erotic. Should this happen, we can play with one of the more advanced practices called "classic sexual conditioning". We'll give a couple of ideas on how this works, although it's explained more in detail in the manual "SEX: The magic of BDSM". The technique of classic sexual conditioning is to condition a feeling with another so that the first ends up triggering the desire in the partner to follow the second one. For instance, if you tell a dog a certain word and afterwards always give it a reward of some kind like a bone or biscuit, it'll end up associating both in such a way that every time it hears that specific word it'll start to water at the mouth and surely jump because it'll be expecting that reward, because it doesn't conceive the possibility of not getting it. The same goes for when we want our partner to get aroused for just getting a specific hug or a special kind of act. If we want him to get excited for just getting a little slap on the buttocks, it's as simple as ALWAYS repeating it in different sexual moments a little slap on the buttocks followed without interruption or with a very short interval between both acts, touching or sucking his member. This way, every time he receives a little slap on the buttocks, he'll put himself in the position ready for his determined "warming up". This technique is also good to arouse a man when he's having a hard time getting it up or when for a certain reason the sexual desire (libido) suddenly drops or the loss of transient and sporadic erections.

On the other hand, we can adopt the **sweet and submissive role**. With this role, we can be a student, an employee, a slave, a prisoner, etc. Here it would be us who obeys orders, doing exactly what our partner tells us to do; when and always we also want to do it, of course. One act that is very common with this role, and what arouses men very much, is that of forcing a woman as long as it's just a game and not going over the limit. We may like to literally get hurt, in which case we move on to the BDSM level; so the most important thing isn't really whether pain is inflicted or not, but the point or limit we don't want to pass. Given that the man takes on the role of superiority, forcing the woman to give him oral sex. We can adopt the role of being the woman that is forced, begging him to free us and pretending like we don't want to have sexual relations with him or perform oral sex. We don't need to be too precise in this section, the man, who is in control on this occasion, will know what to ask from us every single moment, so he'll be completely satisfied. Bearing the limits in mind, and making them clear before we even start anything, will keep everything very satisfactory. One thing must be well explained. We must know the difference of the fact of being forced from just appearing to be so. Rape is not a game to be joked about; one thing is sexual abuse and another is pretending to be, where there is no pain or suffering.

Anyway, as was already mentioned, it's never a bad idea to talk about the limits of both before starting with this sexual game. And above all things: the most important thing is us. We will not permit anyone absolutely to go over our limits. We must be very clear what we are prepared to do and what not, and let's not be afraid or feel embarrassed in leaving everything perfectly clear. Sex is an act to enjoy and on both parts, not only one of them. Let us never ever allow anyone to decide for us nor force us to do anything that we don't want, ever.

For example, some men, when feeling in control of the situation, may want to hold our head and guide us in the movements when doing oral sex. What happens is, due to the fruit of desire and arousement, they sometimes get carried away with the intensity and can hurt us. That's why it's convenient to have some kind of sign to let our partner know that we're not liking it and we want to stop. It's better when it's a sign or a neutral word, like for example, apple or lift a hand. This way we can't confuse it with the role we're playing of the woman who is forced. It's important to have it mentioned beforehand so that later nothing gives way to confusions on either behalf.

Now we're going to mention which are the things that we must bear in mind before the act itself so that there's a good preparation of everything:

- **Articles**: let's not forget to have lubricants on hand and oil with or without pheromones, tissues, water, condoms if we're going to use them, etc. If we're going to use oil for a massage to start off with, it's advisable to use towels on wherever we're going to do it on (couch, bed, etc.). There are also special covers available for such purposes, although it kind of breaks the beauty of the situation and the quality of the moment.
- **Clothes**: Let's try to have everything well prepared without forgetting anything before we begin and pay close attention when the time comes to putting them on, as there are outfits that are somewhat more expensive and with weak, easy-to-break forms of closure.
- **Make-up**: it is recommended to put on our make-up

before we put on the clothes, because if we dress before we may have diffulty in moving. Let's remember to use permanent lipstick or shiny gloss. If mascara is used it is highly recommended that it's waterproof, because it's very easy during oral sex for our man to touch our eyes or we ourselves could brush against his skin. Let's try not to put on excessive make-up, but just enough to look pretty. In the case we play a wilder role we can use black eyeliner, red lipstick and warm tones for the skin. If we want to dress more like a "Lolita" or tender style, a pink eyeshadow with black mascara and pink gloss could be the best option along with light tones for the skin and a light touch of pale pink or peach for the cheeks.

- **Accesssories**: we must be careful when we wear them as some of them are pretty delicate and break very easily as it usually happens with the chain belts. To do good oral sex without any hindrance we recommend to avoid long earrings or long necklaces. If we want to wear something around our neck, better wear one that's more like a choker (there are really nice black ones with little holes and with rheinstones or without).

- **Food-drink**: as we've mentioned before, if we think we're going to feel really shy, we can share a couple of glasses of wine, sangria, etc. with our partner a few minutes before we begin. It's not advisable to drink more than two glasses nor drink anything stronger; it's about loosening up a little and enjoying it; we're not out to loosen up too much nor lose control but totally the opposite. If we want to play with whipped cream, let's make sure we don't leave it out of the fridge after having bought it. If we use fruit, let's try to have it already cut up and kept fresh in the fridge. On the contrary, if we use chocolate, it should be warmed up a bit (about warming up the chocolate, it's better to do it when we're already made up and dressed, being careful obviously of not getting stained, at least not until we're having fun with our partner).

- **Cleanliness**: Let's shower just before we get dressed and prepared. If our partner has to shower and we're ready, we can tell him that we'll wait for him in bed and to please not take too long in the shower, asking him to do it so as to give him a "surprise". Just with this word alone he should be heading for the shower in a hurry. If he doesn't do it, we must insist and tell him clearly that without one there can't be the other (with tact, affection and sweetness, of course, using mellow words of love, because you earn more with a droplet of honey than with a gallon of gall).

12

TRUTHS AND MYTHS

"Sex, then I exist… And then I think, if I remember".

Faregato

Oral sex is bad

Not at all. In some parts of society, certain religious and moral taboos against oral sex still exists, but this is just one more technique when it comes to sexual relations. We must freely experience our sexuality, freeing us from all prejudices that attack us and don't let us enjoy ourselves. While proper precautions are taken and with the consent of both, there is no problem. It's a natural act; the genitals are parts of the body just like the rest. If there is hygiene and consentment from the other person, this is one of the most intimate and beautiful practices that can happen between two people.

HIV can be transmitted through oral sex

While it's true that the risk of getting infected with HIV through oral sex is much lower than other practices, there is the possibility of getting infected. This can happen when we have cold sores or open sores in or on the mouth. The semen comes into contact with our blood through these sores and we can catch it. However, if we have proper oral hygiene, there should be no problem. At any rate, if our partner isn't too well-known and trustworthy, it is always more advisable to use condoms. It is important to know that people who have AIDS can spread it through their blood, their semen, their pre-seminal fluids and in the case of women, also through the vaginal secretions. On the other hand, we shouldn't only worry about HIV; having oral sex with a person who is infected can produce herpes, gonorrhea, syphilis, genital warts (human papilloma virus), amebiasis (intestinal parasites) and A or B Hepititis infection. The only measures for all this are two: when doing oral sex, avoid our partner to ejaculate in our mouth, or use barriers such as condoms, dental dams, condoms cut between the genitals and our mouth, or latex sheets made of natural rubber. If there are any doubts, all these diseases can also be caught through oral anal sex.

Oral sex produces mouth cancer

This is something which isn't all that clear as of yet. It seems that doing oral sex on a person infected with human papilloma virus (HPV) increases the possibilities of having oropharyngeal cancer. However, we can't speak of cause, as there are many other factors that also influence in the appearance of this type of cancer, such as smoking and frequent consumption of alcohol.

The majority of women don't practice oral sex because of hygiene

There are some women ---not the vast majority--- but the

ones that don't like to do oral sex, and this is due to various reasons: it seems immoral or degrading to them, they're afraid of catching some kind of Sexually Transmitted Infection (STI), or it seems dirty or unsanitary. In the case that concerns us, simply by keeping a proper intimate hygiene, the problem would be solved. In the other cases, more research on their prejudices and their fears need to be done and work on them. Just as it took time to get rid of slavery and so women could go to university and vote, changes need process and time. The teachings of oral sex being degrading is part of absolutisms made by various religions (not by the God they pray to, because there is nothing directly written from that source about it), and is something that is gradually changing.

The condom is only necessary in case of vaginal penetration

This statement is completely false. Just as we've seen in previous points, the practice of oral sex also has certain risks, so the use of them protect us from sexually transmitted diseases (STD) such as HIV or HPV, among others.

If the penis is removed before orgasm is reached, there is no risk of infection

The truth is that the pre-seminal fluid can have the HIV virus, however, according to most of the researches made, the quantity isn't enough to transmit it. In any case, before any doubts, it's better to prevent and use a condom or any of the other measures considered above.

The only safe method is the condom

The condom is one of the prophylactics that can be used, but there is also the feminine preservative, the latex sheet or the oral preservatives. Nevertheless, the best method to do oral sex to a man is the condom. For other types of practices, such as anal or scrotum stimulation, we can use other methods such as the latex sheets.

Oral sex substitutes coitus

Not at all, oral sex is just another one of the sexual practices there are. Every couple should decide if it'll be the only and main practice, or if instead, introduce it within a much wider repertoire. Just as we like to change meals simply for the pleasure of it, it's good to expand our practices, and search for new ways and positions to practice, as well as opening up a wide range of possibilities of feeling and giving pleasure.

Food influences in the taste of the body fluids

Absolutely correct. In a section later on, which foods should be left out and which ones will be recommended to eat will be explained so that the semen acquires a more pleasant taste.

It's impossible to get pregnant through oral sex

Even though it seems too obvious, it's never a bad idea to clear up possible doubts. We could never get pregnant by practicing oral sex, not even if we swallow the semen. To get pregnant, the spermatozoa must unite with an ovum, and if we swallow it, the semen goes straight to the intestines. So, the only sexual method for us to get pregnant is the vaginal intercourse.

Oral sex is practiced more in casual encounters

This is true. There is a larger tendency in young people practicing this type of sex, since they want to keep away from the fear of an unwanted pregnancy and mistakenly believe, that they don't run the risk of getting any type of STI. What's more, oral sex turns out to be much more plausible as far as time and space is concerned than the penetration itself. This doesn't mean that it should be used as the main practice in casual encounters or that it should be something secondary in steady relationships. They're only stadistic details that show the tendency of young people going towards quicker practices due to the lack of important information.

13

POSITIONS FOR ORAL SEX

"What would he do if he could live his life all over again?:
Try more positions".
Groucho Marx

The position in which we do oral sex in is one of many that can be changed so as not to fall into monotony and that each occasion should be a unique experience.

In the first place, the one mostly used is the one where the man is standing up or sitting down, and the woman gets on her **knees** in front of him. There is a variation to this position which is known as **Captain Morgan**. It consists in the man standing up, lifting one leg and resting it on a chair or on some kind of higher support. This way, it's easier for us to get to the scrotum and stimulate it. A variation that would be more comfortable for him is **the boss's chair**, sitting on the front half of a chair and us on our knees in front of him. This can be done in the shower with the chair as well, and is something that creates a lot of arousement in men, because water, soap and oral sex come together. Obviously, we shouldn't be using the soap when we're going to lick him, totally the opposite, there shouldn't be any soap at all (in it's place we can use lubricants or edible oils, and leave the soap for the petting he'll want to do on our breasts or other parts of the body). If we use this position, we shouldn't forget to make sure that the chair doesn't end up in poor condition from getting wet. The best in these cases is to leave the shower door or curtain open with warm water or just slightly warm being able to alternate with cold water in case we want to quickly harden our nipples or play in some other way with this. It would be much better.if we can leave the shower head high on the wall without either of the couple having to hold it all the time.

Secondly, we find the popular technique of the **"69"** position. In case someone isn't familiar with this, in this position the woman lies on top of the man but in reverse, permitting the man to be able to stimulate her genitals, at the same time that we have access to his member. Actually, the man can also be on top and the woman on the bottom, but then, it's the man that has the initiative and we lose some control from the intensity and the depth to which the penis enters into our mouth (if the man gets too excited, he could lose a little control and could irritate us unintentionally; it's something to really be aware of when it comes to this position). On the other hand, if we make a small change in the "69" position and instead of lying one on top of the other, we could lie **sideways** and we'd have a new position; it can be very gratifying because by both lying sideways, both of us have the possibility to touch other parts of the body such as the breasts, etc.

Another option is that, with the man **lying down**, we settle ourselves on top of him, at the height of his legs, looking at him. With this posture, if the man spreads his legs a little, we can also stimulate the scrotum. On the other hand, if we want to have free access to his erogenous areas, we can have the man put **his knees bent** over his chest (so that he doesn't get tired of having them up, we can put a blanket on the floor in front of a wall where he can support both feet on it, leaving us space between the wall and his body so we can stimulate it with ease). This way, as we masterbate him, we can stimulate the scrotum and the perineum at the same time with the mouth or vice versa (while we're doing oral sex on the member, we can stimulate the rest with our hands); and, if we're with a man without prejudice or limits, even the anus. Another option we have is that, with the same position we had in the beginning ("lying down" position), we put ourselves on top of one of his legs, just like a **koala** bear. This position allows us while we're doing oral sex to him, we can rub ourselves on his leg, making him notice how aroused and moist we are.

Next would be the **doggy** position, which also has its adjustment to oral sex. On this occasion, it's the man that gets on all fours. We get behind him and from there, do oral sex to him. In addition we can also stimulate his anus, the perineum and the scrotum. However, this position may be uncomfortable for both the man and the woman, so that's why just the same, it would be better to make an adjustment. Instead of being behind our man, we can lie down beneath him, with our head between his knees, at the height of his penis. From there though, we couldn't stimulate other areas as easily, but at least oral sex would be easier.

Another possibility is that we lie down and our man sits **on our chest** (more likely under our breasts), supporting his kness on the bed so as not to put too much pressure on us. In this position, it's the man that has control of the situation, being able to insert the penis how and whenever he wants. However, this could cause problems. It may be that, as a result of excitement at the moment, our partner increases the intensity of his rhythmic jerking, or insert the penis too far in. This is why it's convenient to stipulate some kind of sign so that the man stops in case we feel uncomfortable or if we're choking.

Now to finish, we're going to comment on one of the most delicate positions. It consists of the woman **lying down face up**, placing her head on the edge of the bed, so that the head slightly inclines towards the floor. The man stands in front of us and from there puts his penis in our mouth. The same way as above, you must agree on a signal of some sort to use when wanting to stop in case of choking or annoyance. This position is ideal for practicing the technique known as **"deep throat"**, which consists of introducing the penis entirely into our mouth. If we tried to do this practice in another position, it would possibly be much more complicated and uncomfortable, since the penis would run head on with our throat and would give us a sense of choking and the urge to vomit. From this position, our mouth and throat are aligned, so it's easier for us to insert the penis deeper.

In any case, if we see that we don't feel prepared for these techniques or cause us too much nausea, we can start trying with vibrators so we get more used to having an object of that size in our throat. Nor should we worry too much if we're not able to do this practice or the fact of showing our partner that we're choking. Even though it hardly seems erotic, men get aroused at the thought of it not fitting in our mouth because they have a big member, that makes them feel proud and more manly.

There are as many positions as imagination that we can have. Let's not worry about trying out new things, trying out is how you really find out about the best things in life, so let's not set limits and let the imagination fly and the pleasure with it.

14

DIFFERENCES BETWEEN A CIRCUMCISED PENIS AND ONE THAT ISN'T

"Whichever way you look at it, sex is extremely memorable and satsifying when things go well. Those who handle the sexual aspects in a relationship with skill have an important asset to stimulate romantic love".

Helen Fisher

A circumcised penis, which means a penis without the foreskin, has characteristics and a sensitivity different to the uncircumcised penis. As we go along we'll see some details to bear in mind about each type of penis.

Circumcision is mainly done for religious purposes, but there are also cases in which, due to health problems, it's necessary to operate. One of those cases is phimosis, which consists in the opening of the foreskin not being big enough and doesn't let the glans out, either partially or totally.

One the positive aspects of circumcision is that it allows for a better hygiene of the glans. However, there is no reason why men who haven't been circumcised should have any type of problems in this matter, all they have to do is let the glans out when they shower and keep good hygiene. What's more, it has also been proven that a circumcised penis has a lower risk in catching sexually transmitted infections, this could also explain why the inner part of the foreskin is made of mucous membrane, a membrane where the virus can pass through much easier. If we remove this membrane, infections are less likely to ocurr. However, this doesn't mean that circumcised men are free of risk. They must have the same precautions like the uncircumcised men.

Another of the changes experienced in circumcised men is the loss of hypersensitivity in the glans. When the glans is covered by the foreskin, it is permanently protected and moist. On the other hand, when you remove the foreskin, the glans is uncovered, creating more friction with the clothes and eliminating that moistness. All that causes the loss of that hypersensitivity in the glans. This does not mean that circumcised men feel less pleasure, it just changes the way they feel. Many uncircumcised men feel each little friction that ocurrs in the glans very intensely, so you must be very careful with the stimulation. On the other hand, with the circumcised men, by losing this hypersensitivity, you can play more freely.

However, not all is so positive. By removing the foreskin, you're also removing the nerve endings that could be played with, and in addition, in some circumcisions the frenulum is also removed, which is one of the most sensitive areas and with which you get more pleasure out of.

The uncircumcised men seem to feel more pleasure from the pressure on the head of the penis, hence the oral sex on the tip of the penis being more pleasant. In exchange, circumcised men enjoy the stimulation on the crown of the glans and frenulum, if they have one.

Anyway, whether the penis is circumcised or not, pleasure is equally felt. The only difference we find are in the feelings that are experienced and where they're experienced.

15

EXAMPLES OF
GUIDED ORAL SEX

"The only place we can control a man is in bed. If we would perpetually perform oral sex on men, we could dominate the world".
Samantha Jones, character in Sex in the City

Following are, five oral sex exercises that will be

detailed to serve as a guide and example.

We will also display five different situations with its corresponding method so as to have more options of possibilities. They're all different from each other, so that each one of them is a new exprerience for our man. Although the techniques are similar, the important thing is to keep the arrangement of the steps and its order in mind, the same as its strength and speed. First we can try with some object that resembles it and with it imagine taking all the steps and reviewing them in our spare time. The art of oral sex is achieved when we've practiced the steps on a regular basis. Just like when we learn to swim we must keep each of the things that we have to do first in mind so that later on we'll do it automatically. The magic of the most wonderful and unforgettable oral sex experiences are based on having the steps very clear.

Method 1
With the man lying down, we begin to approach his genitals from the feet up with our head down and looking into his eyes, as if we were a feline animal just about to attack its

prey. When we come to his thighs, we stop. We separate his legs a little so we can see **the inner part of the thighs** better. Next, we start to kiss every inch of his thighs. We can start with a little sucking and, considering that this area allows it, we can also give a little bite but softly. It's not about hurting him, just simply show him that we like to play.

After that we can go on to the **scrotum**. We massage it lightly with one hand and then we proceed to stimulate it with our tongue and mouth. We can put one testicle in the mouth and suck it gently. We repeat "gently" because we already know this area is very sensitive to pain. While with our mouth we're playing with the scrotum, we can stimulate the **perineum** with one of our hands. With our fingers we should press while we're making circular movements at the same time, it's more of a massage rather than a caress.

Once we've finished with these areas, we go on to work his **glans**. Take his penis by the base and with the tongue extended give it a soft lick over the entire glans.

Then we can put it in our mouth and give it a subtle suction. What we want him to know is what he's going to enjoy in a little while and right now he wants to have more.

Next we go to the **base of his penis** and, with the head set perpendicular to his penis, we do a continuous suction, which goes from the base until almost to the glans and so on, from up going down. When we get tired, or after a few repetitions, we give it one lick from the base to the tip of the penis, with our eyes fixed on his. And here is where we begin to really stimulate his glans.

We begin with another soft lick over the entire glans and we play a while on his **frenulum**. With the tongue extended, we give soft licks around the area. Then, we set our lips closed on the tip of the glans and, gradually open them, letting the glans go slowly into our mouth with pressure but making sure that it's lubricated enough (we can lubricate it with our own saliva or with some external help such as etible oil, syrup, etc.). We should put light pressure on it with our lips, so that the sensation is more intense. We must also remember to have our lips moist, so there's no friction with the glans. Once we have the entire glans inside, we do repeated suctions.

We can alternate it with licking the frenulum. To rest for a moment with this movement, we can lick the **crown of the glans**. With the tip of the tongue, we run across the whole area and then, we go back to stimulating the glans as we said earlier.

If we want to rest our mouth or head a bit, we can masterbate our man for a while and then continue with the oral stimulation. If we repeat the stimulation exercises on the glans several times mentioned in the previous paragraph, we'll soon have succeeded getting our man to finish.

Method 2

This time we're going to begin to stimulate a taboo area: the **anus**. If our partner is one of those who doesn't want to hear about even getting near that area, we can go to the next step. However, if our man is daring and open to new experiences, let's go ahead.

On this occasion, so the stimulation is easier, we'll ask our man to lie down face up and pull his knees up to his chest. We can start by stroking the area around the anus with the tip of our finger, making circles. If we lubricate it with saliva, it'll feel better. Then we can continue to lick the area with our tongue. In the same way as before, we can use the tip of our tongue as if it were a finger and run the entire circumference of the anus (remember that there are things that prevent our tongue from directly touching this area).

Next, with the tongue extended we can lick over the anus and gradually work our way up to the **perineum**. In this area we continue licking, going from the anus to the scrotum repeatedly. We can also use the tip of the tongue to massage the area. We can press a little since the perineum isn't as sensitive as other areas. Lastly, we'll do several suctions and then go on to the scrotum.

With the **scrotum** we'll do the same dynamic performance that we've been applying up until now: lickings and suctions. If we want to innovate a bit, there's a vertical groove that divides the scrotum in two. This area is more sensitive, so we can focus on licking this line to offer a different stimulation.

While we're playing with the scrotum, we'll have one hand on the **penis**, doing a gentle masterbation. Gradually, we'll be changing the manual stimulation for the oral one, and the hand that we had on the penis we'll put it on the scrotum to continue massaging the area.

We take the penis with one hand and approach our lips to the **glans**. We then run our moist lips over it as if it were lipstick. We'll intersperse this technique with gentle licking, to then continue with the lip stimulation. Afterwards, we can continue with suctions all around **the base of the penis**, while with one hand stimulating the upper part. It is very important to use lubricant for the hands, otherwise the friction would be too intense for that area.

Later we can go back to stimulating the anus and the perineum with intense licking and strong suctions, so that later, with the man fully prepared, proceed to the grand finale.

To finish, we put one hand on the base of the penis and press lightly, this way the blood will be concentrated in the glans and the sensations will be stronger. Then, we proceed to licking the **frenulum** softly. Later we go on to circle the **crown of the glans** with the tip of the tongue. We repeat both stimulations several times and finish off sucking the glans. Up until now, we've limited ourselves simply to suctions on the glans, however, now we can go a little further and insert the penis half way, making up and down movements with the mouth, simulating what would be a penetration. We'll combine this movement with stimulating the glans only, so that our neck rests and to intensify the pleasure of our man. While we're sucking with the mouth, the tongue can give light taps on the frenulum, so as to increase the sensation and finishes beforehand. We'll be increasing the speed a little more and each time inserting his member a little deeper (being careful not to let it reach the back of the throat as it can produce gagging). When we notice that he's finishing we continue with the exact same speed and the same movements. If we want him to ejaculate outside of our mouth, we can ask him before we begin that when he's near finishing, he'll be responsible to remove it and finish in a determined area wherever we say or wherever he wants.

Method 3

We start kissing our man's neck with soft suctions. We use the tongue to lick sweetly, softly and slowly from the collarbone till the ear passing over his neck with tenderness. Next we go the same way but giving soft and light kisses with the lips. If he likes to have his earlobe licked, we do it softly and whisper tender things in his ear in a soft and low tone. Then we go to his **pectorals** and his **nipples**. Licks, suctions and even soft little bites, are appreciated in this area. Gradually we go lower with the tips of our fingers softly and slowly towards his **lower abdomen**, and then we stay here for a while. Just like with the nipples, we can lick, kiss, suck and a little bite in this area while we run lightly like a feather over his hip and the outer part of his legs with the palm of our hand and the tips of our fingers. We gradually approach his genitals and then move away. One important thing is that, if we have long hair, we should wear it down and subtly, we let our hair fall around his genitals. So, while we're stimulating his abdomen, our hair is stroking his penis. The lower abdomen, being so close to the genitals, is also very erotic, and not because it's very sensitive, but because, given the closeness to the penis, the man anticipates what will happen later. So, playing with this anticipatory thinking, we're going to lower our head by his penis, keeping the look fixed on his eyes. We'll pass our mouth close to his penis, so he can feel our breath, but we'll keep going, without even as much as giving it a small kiss. What we're looking for is to delay touching it directly as much as possible, we want him to beg us for it.

We go on to the stimulation of his **perineum**. To have better access, we can ask him to slightly bend his knees, this way the scrotum rises a little and gives us way to the perineum. We'll start licking this entire area, running the tongue each inch of the way. Gradually we will increase the pressure with the licks we're giving till passing on directly to suction.

Later, we'll go on to licking the scrotum, starting on

the area below and then going upwards, and so on in turn over the entire area. Once we've finished, we can suck one or both testicles.

Then we continue to work on the penis. We'll take it into our hands and, without actually touching it, put the **glans** into our mouth, forming with it an "O" shape. We'll try to make him notice our warm breath. The waiting will make our man despair and succumb into ecstasy. Next, we take the penis out of our mouth and we go down to the **base**. We run our tongue licking the whole penis, till we get to the **frenulum**, where we'll stop for a moment.

We take hold of the penis by its base, with our mouth open and with the tongue extended, we'll give the glans, and in particular the frenulum gentle taps with our tongue. At this point the important thing is not to move our mouth or our tongue, but to guide the member with the hand, moving it towards our tongue, producing clashes with the tongue that can be heard, because they really will be jolts or clashes. Afterwards we'll lick over the frenulum and we then proceed to insert, this time for real, the glans into our mouth. We should cover it completely, the frenulum and the crown should also go inside. In fact, our lips should be at the height of the **crown of the glans**. With our lips we'll press softly on this area, and we will turn our head so that our lips are stimulating the entire lower part of the glans. At the same time, we can lick the glans extensively with our tongue and give gentle taps with the tip of it. Then we will make spiral movements (turn the head to one side and the tongue to the other side or with fast horizontal movements) going down over the whole member, meanwhile we'll be inserting it, going down and then up and repeating the procedure again.

As we've been doing throughout this exercise, we'll continue to play a little with our man's expectations. Therefore, we can pass on to stimulate his frenulum with our tongue, and continue increasing the pace of the licks until we see that he's really getting aroused. Then it's the moment to stop and go lower to stimulate the scrotum. This sudden stop will hit him by surprise, but it'll show him that we are the ones in charge today, we decide when and where to give him pleasure. If we do this, we must remember that stopping delays the moment of the end because it'll almost be like starting from zero. These games help him enjoy it longer, but it also means that we'd have to spend more time satisfying him in order to finish. On the scrotum we can do the same as before, licks or suctions, just until we see that our man's arousement has calmed down a little. This'll be the moment when we'd go back to the penis, this time to finish the job. In this new swoop we can put his member into our mouth, holding it with our hand, we press it against the inner side of the mouth (which would be the cheek but inside the oral cavity), and then we take it out of the mouth with enough pressure to remove it by feeling the pressure and managing to get a sound but without doing any harm. Next we open our mouth and stick our tongue out to tap his member against the tongue from up going down (moving his member, not our tongue which will remain still against the thrusts of his phallus).

As a final point, we'll proceed to suck the glans repeatedly. We'll cover the entire head of the penis with our lips and gently keep slipping it out while we're sucking. And so on successively, increasing the pace of the continuous insertion of the penis and the intensity of the suctions until our man reaches his orgasm.

Method 4

In this method, we begin leading our head from the feet up towards his genitals. When we're near his scrotum, we'll pause and begin to stroke the **inner part of his thighs**, we can also approach our mouth and breathe gently on them or even blow (always going from down upwards) so he knows we're close. We can also use a feather if he's not too sensitive with tickling.

Next we go on to stimulate his **scrotum**, we'll perform several suctions in the area of his testicles while groaning in a guttural and low sound to show him how we enjoy satisfying him and then quickly go on to his penis. This time we'll be more direct, so that there are different methods: some quicker and others more elaborated. What's more, sometimes there's not enough time. This method is handy to surprise him before he goes to work or in situations where there's little time or when we could get caught "in fraganti" if it's in a public place.

We'll begin with taking his penis by the base and tap ourselves with it on the cheek. Then we'll open our mouth and insert the **glans**, rubbing it a bit in the inner wall of our mouth. Next, we go on to masterbate him with the hand, putting our mouth on the top part of the glans at the same time. While our hand is making up and down movements by the **trunk of the penis**, we'll be licking and kissing the glans. At the same time, with the other free hand, we'll stimulate the scrotum, giving it a massage. We can also go on to the **perineum** and give circular or straight line massages, pressing every now and then. One of the keys to connect an act with another which then has him anticipating and getting excessively aroused every time we press on his perineum is; to leave everything else and focus only on the perineum and frenulum or on the perineum and the glans. What we do is press and immediately after (with hardly leaving any time between both) give small taps with the tongue on the frenulum or put our lips over the glans pressing lightly, producing the feeling of penetration. With this, after several repetitions, every time we press on the perineum we'll notice how his penis gets aroused and anticipates or expects the act that we have related or connected.

When we've been doing this dynamic act for a while, we can make a variation. We put both our hands around his penis, and place our mouth on the top part of the glans, next to our hands. We should form something like a channel. Once we're ready, we'll be prepared to move our hands and mouth at the same time and in the same direction, it'll be like feigning a penetration. After a few minutes and with the lubricant handy, we can start to move our hands, each one in one direction and making circular movements in opposite directions. On the other hand, we keep our mouth on the glans, stimulating the **frenulum** and the **crown** with the tongue and lips at the same time.

Lastly, with the channel structure once again, we'll allow our man to be the one who moves the pelvis, feigning the movement of penetration. This technique will serve us to put   the final point to this exercise.

Method 5

On this occasion, we're going to begin from the end, the

penis. We'll begin masterbating our man. Once the penis has a considerable erection, we go on to stimulate his **glans** with our mouth. We'll suck the upper part of the penis several times, making up and down movements all along the penis, masterbating with the mouth.

This will serve as an advance of all that'll come next, but since we don't want our man to finish in two seconds, we'll give him some time to rest. For that, we go on to stimulate the **scrotum** and the **perineum**. While we're licking and sucking the testicles area, we'll be massaging the perineum with one hand. Once we've finished with the scrotum, we go on to stimulate the perineum orally. Here we can apply more intensity and add pressure with the tongue, pressing as if it were a finger. With one hand we can be massaging the **inner part of the thighs** and in the most intense moments, we can slightly dig in our nails, to show how aroused we're getting.

Immediately after, we go back to stimulating the glans. On this occasion, we focus on giving moist kisses on the **frenulum**. After a couple of seconds in this area, we put the glans into our mouth and start with movements going from down upwards, pausing conscientiously when we go by the **crown of the glans**, where we'll apply more pressure and make small turns with the head, to stimulate the entire surface. Immediately afterwards, we run the tongue to the limit between the glans and the rest of the member (the crown), but this time making a couple of turns uninterruptedly and giving no pleasure to any other part of his member.

When we need to stop, whether it's for us to rest or because our guy is getting too aroused, we can continue with the masterbation, while we stimulate his scrotum with our mouth. When we want to get back to the action, we'll get into the appropriate position for the "deep throat" maneuver. Any position is good in which we feel comfortable to introduce the penis all the way down. The most recommended position is to get on top of our man with our back to him, although in this case we won't be able to look at him while we're doing it.

Once we've found our position, we'll proceed to

suctions of the glans, inserting it in a little further each time. We'll be combining quick taps in the suctions of the glans with slower movements in which we introduce the penis half way and adjust the opening of our mouth as well; doing it sometimes with our lips almost closed (and therefore, adding more pressure), and other times open wider to move his member making it bump with the lips and with the inner walls of our mouth as we introduce it. When we feel prepared, we'll insert the penis completely and we hold it like that for a few seconds on some occasions and on others we'll do it slowly till we get to the end, holding it for a second and then backing out slowly as well. If we don't get to the end, we're not to worry about it, we'll just do it as far as we can go without hurting or overwhelming ourselves (practice makes it gradually easier each time). This is a good time to dig in our nails into the thighs and show him our passion (bearing in mind his sensitivities and tastes). On the other hand, if the position allows us, it's very important to keep eye contact with our man, so he can see our effort to insert his entire penis into our mouth which will arouse him very much.

We should keep combining the suctions on the glans with the deep throat insertion, and then rest during periods in which we simply masterbate him. When we notice that our man is already very aroused, we focus on quick suctions on the glans, then running our tongue on the frenulum. If we do all this, he'll reach his orgasm quickly.

These five methods are intended to provide a basic guide so we can offer good oral sex, even though we're not experts or just starting out in this art at these moments. However, it is totally advisable to modify it to our liking and introduce several new things. For example, we can vary the positions, the place, introduce new roles, play with the senses and sensations, etc. Anyway, every man is in a world of his own, so it will be us, with his help and the base of experience, who will get to know what our partner and we ourselves like most. Between our lovers and ourselves we can build our own methods.

16

THINGS YOU SHOULD NEVER TELL A MAN

"The erotic instinct belongs to the original nature of man.
It is related to the highest form of spirit".
Carl G. Jung
"A word strikes deeper than a sword".
Robert Burton

Men tend to focus their manhood and confidence on their physical appearance and above all, on their penis.

That's why we must be very careful when we talk about their member, because an unfortunate comment could hurt their pride and self-esteem.

Comments like: "your penis is a strange color", "it looks like it's bent", "it has a strange shape", "that condom is too big for you" only those women who don't know how to treat men say such things, the ones who haven't discovered the art of the magic sensual-sexual. Unless we think there could be some kind of medical problem, we should leave these thoughts in our mind. On the other hand, we should also be careful with comments about their size. Of course, phrases such as "it's small but cute" should be more than forbidden in our warehouse of phrases. If we want to refer to his penis or its size it should be to lift his self-esteem: "how big it is!", "it's perfect" or "it turns me on!". In any case, it's also important that these compliments have some truth in them, because to praise its large size when he has a small penis would sound very false and, in addition, he could feel that we could be lying about other things too. If his penis is small, better say things such as: "it's ideal for me", "it's the nicest I've seen so far" and "I'm in love with it" or "I love it".

If our man has other **physical complexes**, we shouldn't make any comments or remarks about them either. For example, we should never make comments such as: "well, you're not that strong", "I'm taller than you are", "you should go to the gym", "you're putting on weight" or "you're too hairy". We can follow the same guidelines that we've already mentioned earlier and convert these faults into his strong points. So, if for example our partner has really rough hands or has a lot of body hair, we can make him see that this makes him more manly and that turns us on very much (in case we don't like his body hair, we can get rid of it ourselves with a shaving machine and the excuse that this way he can enjoy the surprise we have prepared for him a lot more). It's about transforming a fault into something positive; this is fundamental in the art of eroticism and sexuality.

Another thing we should keep to ourselves are **comparisons**, and above all if they are about our x-boyfriends. If we want to show him that he's our best lover, that we've never enjoyed it so much with anyone as much as with him, it's best we say it like this: "I've never enjoyed it so much". It's unnecessary to get into comparisons with old boyfriends and even less, of someone in particular. Let's try to make him feel as if he's the only one that's ever come into our life. There isn't and there wasn't anyone else. Our mind is set one hundred per cent since we've met him (obviously this doesn't have to be like this all the time, only while we're witih him).

This section is explaining everything that we shouldn't say to our partner, but there are times when it's necessary to let him know something that can be taken negatively. In these cases, what we can do is use the tecnique called **"sandwich technique"**. It's about saying something negative, but together with something positive which precedes it and another that follows. For instance, we could tell him: "I enjoy sex with you very much, but I'd like to try other more innovative positons, although I also love the ones we usually use as well...".

However, there are times in which we're unable to

polish up what we're trying to say and although we don't want to, we end up hurting our man. In these cases, we can turn to another **alternative**. For example, in the case that we'd like to tell him that his intimate smell bothers us and that's why we don't want to perform oral sex with him, we can get around it with an explanation and ask him to trim his pubic hair a little, since this way it's easier for us to stimulate the intimate areas and what's more, we can also enjoy a better view of his penis which drives us crazy, and we go around it every now and then like "cats on heat". This way we get to eliminate the hair, which is a source of sweat and where most of the odor is impregnated. Another way is to suggest we start with foreplay in the shower, this way we make sure he's clean and then being able to enjoy a wet and warm moment at the same time. In case we don't like the taste of his sperm and wanting to tell him that we won't swallow it, we can turn to another alternative and insert the penis when it's more noticeable just as our partner is going to ejaculate, that way the sperm falls directly into the throat and we avoid it touching our taste buds; or if we don't want him to ejaculate in our mouth, we can tell him that we need for him to come on our breasts, the tummy or any other part (so he feels that it's a necessity for us, that we get very aroused seeing him in front of us and watching the semen come out on our body). Another possible solution is to mention the possibility to him of changing his diet so that the taste of his sperm changes as well, but we'll see about that further on.

We must also bear in mind the **moment in which we have these conversations**. Although it's about sexual matters, we don't want to talk about serious subjects in the middle of sexual relations. It would be very uncomfortable and inappropriate; what's more, it could drop the sexual desire dramatically and even lose the desire all together until several hours have passed after having forgotten those spoken words. So for matters such as, for instance, "set safety limits or signals to take into account according to what practices" or "if he would like for us to stimulate his anus", it would be convenient to talk about it with time and tranquility. Communication in a couple is a fundamental matter, but we must remember to do it gently and above all with mellow sweetness (without overdoing it but not underdoing it either). Men love sweet words, it dazzles them, it makes them fall in love and lose their minds over us. If we know what to say, how and when, we'll have won much more than heaven with them.

17

WHAT TO DO IF HE HAS TROUBLE FINISHING

"The greater the sexual pleasure of man, the greater the happiness of the woman".

Plato

One of the problems that we may have when we perform oral sex is that our man has a lot of trouble reaching an orgasm.

There are several reasons why this can happen. One of them could be our **inexperience**. If we're new at this practice, we do not yet have the necessary skills to know how or where to stimulate our man, although that changes once we practice what we've learned here. Most likely, he isn't receiving enough stimulation, so we would have to focus on working more on the glans and its frenulum, which are the most sensitive areas. We can also help ourselves with visual and sound effects, as mentioned in previous chapters. On the other hand pressure and above all rhythm is very important (learn to go faster in the movements, slowing down if we want it to last longer or going from slow to fast as we're wanting to approach the end).

As it occurs with everything, practice makes perfect. As we go along trying out, we'll gain experience and we'll also get to know which areas are the ones that we need to work on more with our partner.

It can also be that **monotony** has settled in our sexual life, although oral sex is often well received. In any case, we can always try out a new position, take on a new role or change the place where we normally practice oral sex. Regarding positions, an entire chapter has already been devoted to talking about it, so we already have enough ideas to innovate. As far as roles in games are concerned, it has also been widely discussed in a chapter. But we've barely discussed about places where to practice oral sex. Some ideas different from the bed can be: in the shower, in the kitchen, in the car, in the elevator, in a hotel, outside in the open air, etc. It all depends on how daring and playful we are, and if it arouses us to experience the possibility of being discovered or not. To get out of the monotony as such, we can venture to go over the limit and try things that up until now were taboo or unused such as light sadomasochism games, etc.

Finally, another problem that lies behind delayed ejuculation is that he doesn't reach **a full erection**. What can happen when we stop stimulating the penis and pass on to other areas, is that the penis loses firmness. If the penis is partially limp, this tells us that there's not enough blood in the penis, so the sensitivity and pleasure that it could feel would be much less. What we must do in these cases is get all our tools out. First, we focus on stimulating its glans, the crown and the frenulum. At the same time, we press the perineum gently with one hand but clearly pushing downwards, carefully stretching the skin and with this, even slightly lower that of the scrotum (what we're trying to do is tense up the skin of the scrotum, so that a slight tension is noticed). Once we get his member to the desired firmness, we can get a hold of the base of the penis with one hand so that it's more difficult for the blood to leave the area. You don't have to push too hard either, we don't want to squeeze it, getting a hold of the penis with firmness is enough. With all of this under control, we can try to stimulate other areas or continue directly with the stimulation of the penis and finish quickly. It's essential to help ourselves with mellow words and groans and exhale our breath on sensitive areas where we've licked previously. We must remember that the arousement should end in his genitals, not begin there (one of the main errors of the beginners). It's very important to know what to say, when and above all how. Also the kind of groans there are and how to use force according to the area of his body we're at or what we want to get at that precise moment from our lover.

Sudden impotence (Brewer's droop) is one of the things that we can find most regarding this issue. This impotence is temporary that ocurrs while the penis is erect and suddenly goes limp without any apparent cause. It's a sudden disappearance of the erection or not being able to get one at the desired moment. It also tends to happen when erections are only partial. Although it's something common and normal (generally, more than half of the men have experienced this at some time or other or it will happen to them sometime in the future), it's often a source of embarrassment for the man because with it he perceives it as a lack of manhood. The origin of sudden impotence can be one of the following reasons among others: stress, fear of failing in the act, too self-demanding, insecurity of his appearance or achievement of the act, fear of getting a woman pregnant, low sexual appetite, feeling guilty, lack of prolonged sleep, recurring thoughts in the mind, over-worked, lack of interest in the partner and inadequate sexual information. We've quoted the most common ones. We can differentiate between physical and psychological causes.

The physical ones include alcoholism, smoking, arterial and hormonal factors, among others. The psychological ones can include financial, professional, education and family problems along with stress, anxiety or depression. What can also enter into this group is the feeling of guilt for having been unfaithful, repressed feelings by sexual tastes and insecurities, lack of interest in the partner or lack of stimulation that is necessary to produce arousal which leads to erection.

What can we do if our man ensues a sudden impotence? Well, the solution depends on the cause itself.

-       **Psychological causes**: if the reasons are nerves, insecurity, pressure or stress, it can be solved with relaxation techniques such as giving him a complete massage that includes the back, legs and arms. In these cases sex should be left for last and go from down upwards approaching steadily closer to the intimate areas without touching and when we get there, do so very little and lightly, as if by mistake. This should be done until our partner decides to get on with it. If he should prefer to sleep, we should let him do so. When he gets up he will have rested as he needed and will surely be ready to enjoy sex with us. We can also choose to exercise or spend an hour or two with a hobby our partner likes the most. Sometimes all that's needed is to clear the mind.

- **Physical causes**: (alcohol, drugs, poor diet...): in this case the only choice we have is to talk with our partner about the necessity of changing certain habits (in these cases, especially regarding alcohol or drugs, we have to be very tactful because these are difficult issues even for psychotherapies). Cases based on physical causes can be much better dealt with from a professional point of view.

How to know the difference between sudden impotence ("Brewer's droop") and sexual impotence? Sudden impotence happens in precise and temporary situations, while sexual impotence is a lack of erection on a continuous basis. In the latter case it is absolutely necessary to go see a specialist and maintain the treatment that they advise us on a continuous basis. In any case, the lack of an erection or a sudden droop is considered normal if it doesn't affect more than 50% of all intercourses together; Which means to say that if this has happened only on some occasions, it's absolutely normal.

The most important in these cases is to talk with tenderness and reassure our partner that he is what's most important to us, and of course, anything that he might consider a problem can be overcome in one way or another. What's more, although he can't get erections, he can enjoy caresses and pampering while the problem is being taken care of.

This chapter is about the man who has a difficult time to finish because of a lack of stimulation or because the technique isn't being done well. Nevertheless, it could also happen if the problem is medical or psychological, for example if they were going through a time of a lot of stress or having problems at work. However, if we understand that it is a specific problem and our man with other sexual practices has a healthy erection and succeeds to ejaculate at the time desired, we can disregard these pathologies. Anyway, if there is any doubt, it's best to contact a professional specialist.

There are also natural and artificial substances that help to get an erection, however, we strongly recommend to talk to a doctor specialized in these matters.

18

IMPORTANT THINGS NEVER MENTIONED IN OTHER BOOKS ABOUT ORAL SEX

"Sex is the greatest thing that can exist; to be able to feel it, it is necessary to know how to love".

Martin De La R. R

Many compromised and problematic situations

aren't mentioned in other books, whether it's because they're considered obvious, they don't fall into the account of their existence or simply because they're considered vulgar and prefer not to outline any explication. Throughout this last chapter, some of these will be mentioned.

Sometimes, after doing oral sex for a while, with the head movements it involves, **nasal secretion** may appear. This doesn't happen to all women, but to the majority of the women it does; and the more we exert ourselves or do oral sex continuously for a length of time, the more possibility there is of secretion. We don't need to be ashamed of it, just to have a handkerchief on hand will do just in case. When it happens, we can clean our nose using the handkerchief with one hand while with the other we continue giving pleasure to our man by masterbating him. From the moment our nose starts to run, in order to avoid embarrassment that he might see us with a runny or drippy nose, we can change our position where he can't see us in that state (for example, with our back next to him or sitting astride on top of him also with our back to him). What's more, doing oral sex doesn't mean starting to use the mouth on his genitals and staying there until he's finished; totally the opposite, we are the ones who decide how long we keep going and when we're in that area. We can alternate with the hand.

Another problem that can arise with the continuous movement of the head, especially if we're beginners, is **pain in the neck**. When we begin to notice aches, we can change positions or go on to stimulate another area. If what we want is to rest the mouth we can go on to use our hand, and masterbate him or massge the scrotum and the perineum. If on the contrary we have a headache, sore mouth and hands, we can tell him that we got so aroused that we need him to penetrate us. With this strategy, our man won't notice our little problem, we'll rest and what's more, both will reach an orgasm. If he complains, all we have to do is approach him like a little cat on heat and start to whisper in his ear sweet and slowly how we want him to penetrate us, position, speed (if we want him to start slowly or do it at his own speed) and between words groan a little and very quietly.

One thing that worries a lot of woman and is rarely

dealt with is **where to ejaculate**. To explain this explicitly and clearly, there are men who's semen has an unpleasant taste and it's normal that there are women who don't want to swallow it or that her man ejaculates in her mouth. Nevertheless, if the only hindrance is how it tastes, there is a way to change that. To get the semen to be more pleasant, we recommend him to drink plenty of water, to eat citric or sweet fruit –such as apples, melon or mango--, to reduce drinking coffee and alcohol, and avoid sharp foods, garlic, onions and asparagus. If our man follows these guidelines in his diet, the sperm taste will probably improve quite a bit.

Another way to avoid swallowing it is to spit it out. It's not necessary to show signs of repulsion or disgust, we simply take a tissue that we have on hand and spit out the semen there. We can also go to the bathroom for a moment, wash out our mouth and use mouthwash afterwards.

The other issue is when we don't want him to ejaculate in our mouth for other reasons, such as it disgusts us or we think it's dirty. In this case, we should let him know our position before we begin, because it turns men on a lot at the thought of coming in our mouth and we don't want any surprises in the last minute. The same as there are also men who don't like to be kissed after having swallowed his semen and having had it in the mouth, so that's why, if we want kisses in the end, it's best that our man ejaculates elsewhere, or as mentioned before, go to the bathroom to wash out our mouth and then return to his arms knowing that he won't reject our kisses.

As an alternative, if we decide for him to finish outside of our mouth, we can choose another place where it also arouses us. If we're playing a submissive role, we can tell our partner to come wherever he wants on our body. On the other hand, if we're the ones in control, we'll tell him what part of our body we want him to come on. Some areas that are also erotic to ejaculate on are the breasts, the face, the back, the pubic mound or the vagina itself.

Another issue that tends to be a problem is putting his hands **on our head** while we're performing oral sex. Some men like to press the head of their partner towards the penis and guide the rhythm as well as the intensitiy. However, sometimes, due to the arousal of the moment, they can get carried away with impulse and do harm. That's why it's convenient to establish a signal so that the man knows if he can or not put his hands on our head, since there might be days when, due to our state of arousal or submission, we might feel like letting our partner guide us; and other days it might seem uncomfortable.

The most important of all in satisfying the area south of Loira (which was one of the ways that the art of oral sex was called by a French prolific inventor of literature named Frederic Dard) is that we feel comfortable with all that we do. It's interesting trying out new things and have new experiences, but if there is something that we don't want to try out or, once we've tried we realized that we didn't like it, there's no reason why we should do it. Nobody should pressure us, nor should we feel obligated to do so. Our aim here is to give our man pleasure, but never at the cost of our integrity and our well being.

About our own hair removal: we might think that it's not something that's really important, but, to see what men really like and being interested in satisfying them to the max, we should know that always and without any exceptions, they prefer a woman well groomed and hair removed. Even though they tell us the opposite so as not to make us feel bad or to not feel attacked by our recriminations, they always prefer the pubic area well trimmed, as well as the rest of the body like underarms and legs well shaven and at the time of oral sex is no exception, because we're showing him our body and letting him play with it as well, except for the moments within the game where he can't see or touch us.

STD: if we want to know if our partner may have a sexual transmission disease, there have been countless cases (apparently the exception is complete sincerity) where men DON'T tell the truth and don't admit they have sexual transmission disease or infections they have or might have had for fear that we'd stop having sexual relations with them, and especially oral sex. The conclusion we want to reach is, that many times it's better to be cautious than let ourselves be led by the heat of the moment or afraid of losing our partner by asking for something more serious, and then cry at realizing that they've transmitted the infection or disease. So, the best thing to do is ask for medical tests that confirm what he's telling us, and meanwhile, use condoms or other methods already mentioned in other chapters.

Music: at the sexual moment we can choose to play it or not, depending how we feel. If we're beginners or very shy, it could be a good way to relax us. The music most recommended is the kind that reflects eroticism and relaxing at the same time, and they're usually searched for with the following words: ambience, smooth jazz, erotic music, saxophone and piano, etc. If we're looking for a little more excitement, we can play music that includes Arabic touches and groans.

19

THE MOST IMPORTANT THING

"Sex has no sex, only feelings".
The Caris

In this chapter we will talk about the most important factor, which refers to ourselves.

Self-esteem

When we have a low self-esteem we're vulnerable and we

can even feel bad about our body. It's important to feed our self-esteem everyday independently from the person we're with. We must remember that we're born alone and die alone; the only person that exclusively accompanies us throughout our whole life is us, so let's not neglect the most important thing. We're first, and the rest can be seen to calmly afterwards.

Let's not allow for any comments to affect us negatively. In the first place, it's very easy to misunderstand another person, because we don't usually express with words exactly what we want to say. On the other hand, one opinion is not that of everyone else.

Know how to say NO

Sexual practices are being learned as well as strengthened over time and while being practiced or repeated. Tastes and the use of our own sexuality keep changing with us everyday and that is why the practices that we might not like in the beginning, could just as well come to please us someday. Nevertheless, although it's good to have an open mind and innovate, it's also essential to keep in mind that, if we're not prepared for something, it's better not to force ourselves nor let anyone force us or make us feel bad for not going ahead. So, sincerity and respect are necessary in a sexual relationship. Let's not be afraid to say or clearly expose what we're not ready for yet. The other person will understand if they love us and/or respect us. If not, it's better to look for another type of person, because otherwise they'll only hurt us with their selfishness undermining our integrity.

Feeling pretty

We are taught to make ourselves up or dress according to fashion, according to "what will they say" and in looking to satisfy the perception that we give to others. In the century in which we live, we know very well that the first impression of the person is the one we're all left with for life. Even though we don't remember them consciously, the subconscious doesn't forget. Therefore, if it is true that it is advisable to always dress well and/or made up (of course, here is also the possibility of not using any make-up, according to the need, the moment and situation) for the occasion. Good impressions always help in any ambience, whether it's work, school, etc. However, apart from what was mentioned, it must be pointed out, although all this is very good, the main search is ignored and it shouldn't be. The first thing we should really look for is our own satisfaction, feel good ourselves independently whether others will like us or stop liking us; looking for a connection between composure and our tastes. It's a dance that we create with our appearance trying to cover our emotions when we see ourselves in the mirror, when walking, talking, looking, etc., and how others will perceive us (in this case especially, our partner). We should never dress for someone else nor make ourselves up for someone else nor spend money on treatments for another person. We must do it for ourselves, to feel pretty, feel satisfied and feel good. Feeling like this and looking for inner joy, is when we can share it with others feeling fulfilled inside. There's nothing worse than feeling empty. So, first ourselves, and when we feel fulfilled and happy for being who we are, is when we can share such feelings, thoughts and emotions with whoever we decide.

Falling in love

Be careful!! If our lover doesn't want to get serious with us but we're beginning to feel stronger emotions than just the physical attraction, perhaps we should reconsider giving him the best of us, considering that the more we give, the more we'll suffer. We'd know if he really feels something for us when he wants to share as much time as possible with us, when he doesn't make excuses to please us, when he gives it all for us, when he doesn't set limits for our pleasure, etc. In case we're not very clear with this, we shouldn't hesitate to ask him straight out. And attention!! Because guys can be more devious than us. If a man loves us he will clearly tell us. If he doesn't love us he'll make up a thousand excuses so not to hurt us but he'll leave us confused just the same because we won't clearly know what he really feels. Excuses tend to be a NO in disguise 99% of the times.

- I need time
- I need to be alone
- We're different
- I'm not prepared for a relationship

- You need someone who really loves you
- You're too perfect and it scares me
- Comittments scare me
- I need new experiences
- I'm confused because I don't know what I want
- Now I'm in a very delicate professional moment
- I've been really involved in different relationships and I've realized I haven't had any time for myself
- I've just got out of a long relationship
- I'm really tied up at work
- I don't even have time for myself
- I'm constantly traveling and it's not compatible with a relationship

Anything that is priority to us means that he doesn't really love us. It hurts, yes; but it's better to understand the truth and get over it and look for someone who really loves us if that's what we're looking for. If our lover is up to our standards and gives us what we give him, perfect. If not, let's not embitter our lives over it, there are millions of men and life is not meant to be spent crying but to enjoy it to its fullest capacity possible. Let's remember when someone really loves us, they wouldn't let anything interfere, and of course, always would prefer to be with us than somewhere else. Most men would never tell us clearly that they don't love us, so the only thing left to do is divide men into two groups to see things clearly:

Man type 1: he loves me because he clearly told me so and comes after me, leaves everything else in second place with me always as priority (except, of course, within his working hours or outings planned with his own friends).

Man type 2: he tells me things that make me doubt whether he loves me or not. I think he might end up loving me. Tension arises when I ask him what he feels for me. He makes me understand that he does feel something for me (attention, when someone feels "something", it's not enough, it's just an another excuse and just to enjoy the other person until the real love of the their life appears, which obviously is not us).

The important thing is what we want and see if our

partner can give it to us; and even more important is, if he wants to give it to us because that's the way he feels. As we've already said, to give is a beautiful thing, but if the person who receives what we give doesn't feel the same as we do, our spirit will end up wearing itself out together with our self-esteem.

Self-satisfaction

Although we want to give our partner the best of pleasures, we also have a right to enjoy it. We can please ourselves while we're giving it to him too or we can ask him specifically if we don't see him as the initiative. We shouldn't be afraid to ask him; if he doesn't want to give it to us, we'd have one reason more than enough to leave and not see him again, because he who receives should also give, the same as when he gives also has the right to receive.

If we want to satisfy ourselves at the same time that we're giving oral sex to our man, we can use both of our hands, use a dildo, a vibrator or a clitoris massager. The latter is more than recommendable; there are those with different speed functions and are a way for us to finish rapidly. This is interesting since we can get an orgasm at the same time with our partner once we've practiced enough. It's simple and there are even portable and small ones to take in your handbag. It's a highly recommendable product.

If by chance we have a sexual partner who's somewhat lazy in the sense that when he's finished, he doesn't look to see what is left yet to satisfy us, we can take turns. First we can start and then tell him that we're going to need warming up for about five minutes to carry on. As he'll want us to continue with him, he won't be able to resist. We must remember that when we're giving oral sex we're the ones in control and the one to make decisions (unless, we've decided to take on the submissive role), and if he doesn't want to satisfy us, then there's no reason why we should continue doing anything further. Another thing we should never forget under any circumstances is that: "a drop of honey attracts more flies than a gallon of honey", so tenderness, sweet words and mellow treatment should never be left out to get what we want. Men become dumbfounded when they're facing a mellow and sweet girl so, let's use all the aces in the cards in our favor.

20

MAGIC

"Magic is a bridge that permits to go from the visible world towards the invisible and learn the lessons from both worlds".

Paulo Coelho

Magic is an energy so powerful that it's able to achieve almost everything that we can wish for. It has a group of practices and important wisdom, and it's the unity of all these things that makes everything possible and that we get the other person to think, feel or maintain the emotion that we want at that precise moment. Magic is among other things a way to talk, to look, to walk, to touch, the groans, the words, and above all, the details. Magic manages to unite the earthly things with the people's soul, which means to say, what they feel physically with what they feel spiritually.

The practices cover speed, pressure, tenderness, vividness, insight, the use of personality itself, the use of psychology understanding how it's going to affect in a short or long period of time every and each of the things that we do directly as well as indirectly towards the other person, including what can be observed in us that has nothing to do with the other person.

Magic is the true art of knowing how to move and how to act in each situation, to cause one or the other effect. It's deciding what we want to achieve, and carry it out, to grant us the pleasure of enjoying it.

All of us women have this magic inside of us, all we need to do is discover it and enjoy it. We'll see how powerful it is when we begin to use it. It's important to understand that magic can be used to achieve things that are very different, how to make someone fall in love or make him go crazy without falling in love for example. The technique and understanding the psychological framework that's behind it will be the potential base to get what we propose.

AUTHOR`S FACEBOOK:

https://www.facebook.com/SaraBurilloMolinero/?
fref=ts

AUTHOR`S CONTACT:

ansiedadqama@gmail.com

saraburillomoliner@gmail.com

OTHER AUTHOR`S BOOKS:

→ How to attract, seduce, captivate and influence others

→ Anxiety, Somebody help me!!

→ Discover your talent, make it your business

→ Kybalion: Discover the Law of Attraction

→ GODDESS of SEX: Drive your man crazy (under the pseudonym "Dylan Summers")

<u>NOTES</u>

NOTES

Dylan Summers

<u>NOTES</u>

Printed in Great Britain
by Amazon

85976539R10105